Getting Started with Processing

Casey Reas and Ben Fry

D0067710

O'REILLY®

BEIJING · CAMBRIDGE · FARNHAM · KÖLN · SEBASTOPOL · TOKYO

Getting Started with Processing
by Casey Reas and Ben Fry

Published by O'Reilly Media, Inc.
1005 Gravenstein Highway North, Sebastopol, CA 95472

O'Reilly books may be purchased for educational, business, or sales promotional use. Online editions are also available for most titles (*http://my.safaribooksonline.com*). For more information, contact our corporate/institutional sales department: 800-998-9938 or *corporate@ oreilly.com*.

Print History: June 2010: First Edition.

Editor: Brian Jepson
Development Editor: Tom Sgouros
Production Editor: Rachel Monaghan
Copyeditor: Nancy Kotary
Proofreader: Rachel Monaghan
Compositor: Nancy Kotary
Indexer: Ron Strauss
Illustrations: Casey Reas and Ben Fry
Cover Designer: Karen Montgomery

ISBN: 978-1-449-37980-3
[LSI]

[2011-09-16]

Advance Praise for *Getting Started with Processing*

"Making a computer program used to be as easy as turning it on and typing one or two lines of code to get it to say, 'Hello.' Now it takes a 500+-page manual and an entire village. Not anymore. This little book by Ben and Casey gets you computationally drawing lines, triangles, and circles within minutes of clicking the 'download' button. They've made making computer programs humanly and humanely possible again—and that's no small feat."

—John Maeda,
President of Rhode Island School of Design

"*Getting Started with Processing* is not only a straightforward introduction to basic programming—it's fun! It almost feels like an activity workbook for grownups. You may want to buy it even if you never thought you were interested in programming, because you will be."

—Mark Allen,
Founder and Director, Machine Project

"This is an excellent primer for those wanting to dip their feet into programming graphics. Its learning by doing approach makes it particularly appropriate for artists and designers who are often put off by more traditional theory first approaches. The price of the book and the fact that the Processing environment is open source makes this an excellent choice for students."

—Gillian Crampton Smith,
Fondazione Venezia Professor of Design, IUAV University of Venice

"Processing changed dramatically the way we teach programming and it's one of the major factors of the success of Arduino."

—Massimo Banzi,
Cofounder of Arduino

"Casey Reas and Ben Fry champion the exciting power of programming for creatives in *Getting Started with Processing*, a hands-on guide for making code-based drawings and interactive graphics. Reas and Fry are clear and direct, but as artists, they're not afraid to be a bit eccentric and offbeat. This makes their unique form of teaching powerful."

—Holly Willis,
Director of Academic Programs,
Institute for Multimedia Literacy, School of Cinematic Arts, USC

Contents

Preface

We created Processing to make programming
interactive graphics easier. We were frustrated
with how difficult it was to write this type of
software with the programming languages we
usually used (C++ and Java) and were inspired
by how simple it was to write interesting
programs with the languages of our childhood
(Logo and BASIC). We were most influenced
by Design By Numbers (DBN), a language
created by our research advisor, John Maeda,
which we were maintaining and teaching at
the time.

Processing was born in spring 2001 as a brainstorming session on a sheet
of paper. Our goal was to make a way to sketch (prototype) the type of
software we were working on, which was almost always full-screen and
interactive. We were searching for a better way to test our ideas easily
in code, rather than just talking about them or spending too much time
programming them in C++. Our other goal was to make a language for
teaching design and art students how to program and to give more technical students an easier way to work with graphics. The combination is a
positive departure from the way programming is usually taught. We begin
by focusing on graphics and interaction rather than on data structures
and text console output.

Processing experienced a long childhood; it was alpha software from
August 2002 to April 2005 and then public beta software until November
2008. During this time, it was used continuously in classrooms and by
thousands of people around the world. The language, software environment, and pedagogy around the project were revised continuously

during this time. Many of our original decisions about the language were reinforced and many were changed. We developed a system of software extensions, called *libraries*, that have allowed people to expand Processing into many unforeseen and amazing directions. (There are now over 100 libraries.) On November 29, 2008, we launched the 1.0 version of the software. After seven years of work, the 1.0 launch signified stability for the language.

Now, nine years after its origin, Processing has grown beyond its original goals, and we've learned how it can be useful in other contexts. Accordingly, this book is written for a new audience—casual programmers, hobbyists, and anyone who wants to explore what Processing can do without getting lost in the details of a huge textbook. We hope you'll have fun and be inspired to continue programming. This book is just the start.

While we (Casey and Ben) have been guiding the Processing ship through the waters for the last nine years, we can't overstate that Processing is a community effort. From writing libraries that extend the software to posting code online and helping others learn, the community of people who use Processing has pushed it far beyond its initial conception. Without this group effort, Processing would not be what it is today.

How This Book Is Organized

The chapters in this book are organized as follows:

» Chapter 1, "Hello": Learn about Processing.

» Chapter 2, "Starting to Code": Create your first Processing program.

» Chapter 3, "Draw": Define and draw simple shapes.

» Chapter 4, "Variables": Store, modify, and reuse data.

» Chapter 5, "Response": Control and influence programs with the mouse and the keyboard.

» Chapter 6, "Media": Load and display media including images, fonts, and vector files.

» Chapter 7, "Motion": Move and choreograph shapes.

» Chapter 8, "Functions": Build new code modules.

» Chapter 9, "Objects": Create code modules that combine variables and functions.

» Chapter 10, "Arrays": Simplify working with lists of variables.

» Chapter 11, "Extend": Learn about 3D, image export, and reading data from an Arduino board.

Who This Book Is For

This book is written for people who want a casual and concise introduction to computer programming, who want to create images and simple interactive programs. It's for people who want a jump start on understanding the thousands of free Processing code examples and reference materials available online. *Getting Started with Processing* is not a programming textbook; as the title suggests, it will get you started. It's for teenagers, hobbyists, grandparents, and everyone in between.

This book is also appropriate for people with programming experience who want to learn the basics of interactive computer graphics. *Getting Started with Processing* contains techniques that can be applied to creating games, animation, and interfaces.

Conventions Used in This Book

The following typographical conventions are used in this book:

» *Italic:* Used to indicate new terms and filenames, as well as within paragraphs to refer to program elements such as variable or function names, data types, and keywords.

» `Constant width:` Used for program listings.

NOTE: This type of paragraph signifies a general note.

Using Code Examples

This book is here to help you get your job done. In general, you may use the code in this book in your programs and documentation. You do not need to contact us for permission unless you're reproducing a significant portion of the code. For example, writing a program that uses several chunks of code from this book does not require permission. Selling or distributing a CD-ROM of examples from O'Reilly books does require permission. Answering a question by citing this book and quoting example code does not require permission. Incorporating a significant amount of example code from this book into your product's documentation does require permission.

We appreciate, but do not require, attribution. An attribution usually includes the title, author, publisher, and ISBN. For example: "*Getting Started with Processing*, by Casey Reas and Ben Fry. Copyright 2010 Casey Reas and Ben Fry, 978-1-449-37980-3."

If you feel your use of code examples falls outside fair use or the permission given here, feel free to contact us at *permissions@oreilly.com*.

How to Contact Us

Please address comments and questions concerning this book to the publisher:

O'Reilly Media, Inc.
1005 Gravenstein Highway North
Sebastopol, CA 95472
800-998-9938 (in the United States or Canada)
707-829-0515 (international or local)
707-829-0104 (fax)

We have a web page for this book, where we list errata, examples, and any additional information. You can access this page at:

» *http://oreilly.com/catalog/0636920000570*

To comment or ask technical questions about this book, send email to:

» *bookquestions@oreilly.com*

For more information about our books, conferences, Resource Centers, and the O'Reilly Network, see our website at:

» *http://oreilly.com*

Safari® Books Online

 Safari Books Online is an on-demand digital library that lets you easily search over 7,500 technology and creative reference books and videos to find the answers you need quickly.

With a subscription, you can read any page and watch any video from our library online. Read books on your cell phone and mobile devices. Access new titles before they are available for print, and get exclusive access to manuscripts in development and post feedback for the authors. Copy and paste code samples, organize your favorites, download chapters, bookmark key sections, create notes, print out pages, and benefit from tons of other time-saving features.

O'Reilly Media has uploaded this book to the Safari Books Online service. To have full digital access to this book and others on similar topics from O'Reilly and other publishers, sign up for free at *http://my.safaribooksonline.com*.

Acknowledgments

We thank Brian Jepson for his great energy, support, and insight. Nancy Kotary, Rachel Monaghan, and Sumita Mukherji gracefully carried the book to the finish line.

Tom Sgouros made a thorough edit of the book and David Humphrey provided an insightful technical review.

We can't imagine this book without Massimo Banzi's *Getting Started with Arduino* (O'Reilly). Massimo's excellent book is the prototype.

A small group of individuals has, for years, contributed essential time and energy to Processing. We thank Florian Jenett for his web hacking and excellent design ability, Andreas Schlegel for creating the infrastructure for building and documenting contributed libraries, and Dan Shiffman for writing amazing examples and managing the online tutorials. Over time, many others have contributed to the Processing software itself, among them Karsten Schmidt, Eric Jordan, and Jonathan Feinberg. The work of the Discourse forum administrators PhiLho, Cedric, and antiplastik is crucial for keeping the discussion running.

We're amazed by the incredible work of the individuals who write libraries and contribute their work to the community. Thank you to all! A special notice is deserved for Andres Colubri's GLGraphics and GSVideo libraries, Damien Di Fede's Minim sound library, and Karsten Schmidt's extensive and inspiring toxiclibs.

The Processing 1.0 release was supported by Miami University and Oblong Industries. The Armstrong Institute for Interactive Media Studies at Miami University funded the Oxford Project, a series of Processing development workshops. These workshops were made possible through the hard work of Ira Greenberg. These four-day meetings in Oxford, Ohio, and Pittsburgh, Pennsylvania, enabled the November 2008 launch of Processing 1.0. Oblong Industries funded Ben Fry to develop Processing during summer 2008; this was essential to the release.

This book grew out of teaching with Processing at UCLA. Chandler McWilliams has been instrumental in defining these classes. Casey thanks the undergraduate students in the Department of Design Media Arts at UCLA for their energy and enthusiasm. His teaching assistants have been great collaborators in defining how Processing is taught. Hats off to Tatsuya Saito, John Houck, Tyler Adams, Aaron Siegel, Casey Alt, Andres Colubri, Michael Kontopoulos, David Elliot, Christo Allegra, Pete Hawkes, and Lauren McCarthy.

OpenProcessing has emerged as the place to share open source Processing code. We thank Sinan Ascioglu for this amazing community resource.

Processing.js is an exciting future for Processing and the open Web. Three cheers for John Resig, Al MacDonald, David Humphrey, and the Seneca College's Centre for Development of Open Technology (CDOT), Robert O'Rourke, and the Mozilla Foundation.

Through founding the Aesthetics and Computation Group (1996–2002) at the MIT Media Lab, John Maeda made all of this possible.

1/Hello

Processing is for writing software to make images, animations, and interactions. The idea is to write a single line of code, and have a circle show up on the screen. Add a few more lines of code, and the circle follows the mouse. Another line of code, and the circle changes color when the mouse is pressed. We call this *sketching* with code. You write one line, then add another, then another, and so on. The result is a program created one piece at a time.

Programming courses typically focus on structure and theory first. Anything visual—an interface, an animation—is considered a dessert to be enjoyed only after finishing your vegetables, usually several weeks of studying algorithms and methods. Over the years, we've watched many friends try to take such courses and drop out after the first lecture or after a long, frustrating night before the first assignment deadline. What initial curiosity they had about making the computer work for them was lost because they couldn't see a path from what they had to learn first to what they wanted to create.

Processing offers a way to learn programming through creating interactive graphics. There are many possible ways to teach coding, but students often find encouragement and motivation in immediate visual feedback. Processing's capacity for providing that feedback has made it a popular way to approach programming, and its emphasis on images, sketching, and community is discussed in the next few pages.

Sketching and Prototyping

Sketching is a way of thinking; it's playful and quick. The basic goal is to explore many ideas in a short amount of time. In our own work, we usually start by sketching on paper and then moving the results into code. Ideas for animation and interactions are usually sketched as storyboards with notations. After making some software sketches, the best ideas are selected and combined into prototypes (Figure 1-1). It's a cyclical process of making, testing, and improving that moves back and forth between paper and screen.

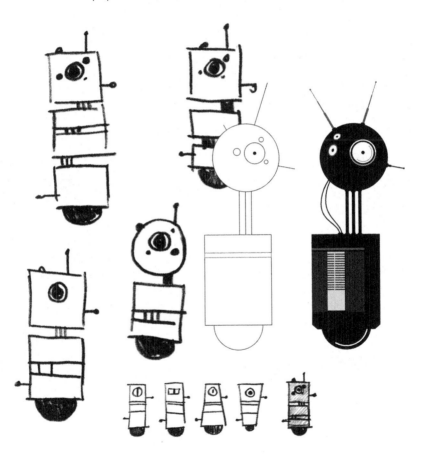

Figure 1-1. As drawings move from sketchbook to screen, new possibilities emerge.

Flexibility

Like a software utility belt, Processing consists of many tools that work together in different combinations. As a result, it can be used for quick hacks or for in-depth research. Because a Processing program can be as short as one line or as long as thousands, there's room for growth and variation. More than 100 libraries extend Processing even further into domains including sound, computer vision, and digital fabrication (Figure 1-2).

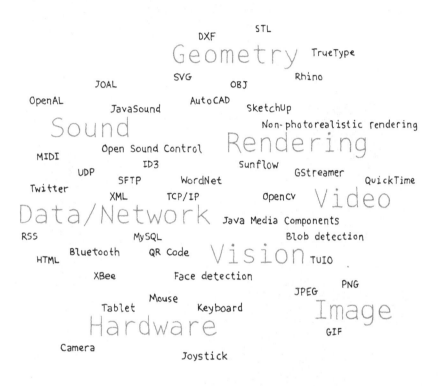

Figure 1-2. Many types of information can flow in and out of Processing.

Giants

People have been making pictures with computers since the 1960s, and there's much to be learned from this history (Figure 1-3). In life, we all stand on the shoulders of giants, and the titans for Processing include thinkers from design, computer graphics, art, architecture, statistics, and the spaces between. Have a look at Ivan Sutherland's *Sketchpad* (1963), Alan Kay's *Dynabook* (1968), and the many artists featured in Ruth Leavitt's *Artist and Computer*[1] (Harmony Books, 1976). The ACM SIGGRAPH archives provide a fascinating glimpse into the history of graphics and software.

Figure 1-3. Processing was inspired by great ideas and individuals over the last four decades.

---

[1] http://www.atariarchives.org/artist/

Family Tree

Like human languages, programming languages belong to families of related languages. Processing is a dialect of a programming language called Java; the language syntax is almost identical, but Processing adds custom features related to graphics and interaction (Figure 1-4). The graphic elements of Processing are related to PostScript (a foundation of PDF) and OpenGL (a 3D graphics specification). Because of these shared features, learning Processing is an entry-level step to programming in other languages and using different software tools.

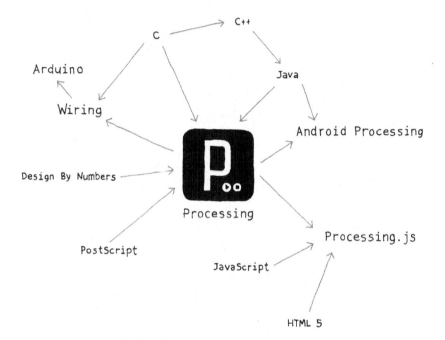

Figure 1-4. Processing has a large family of related languages and programming environments.

Join In

Thousands of people use Processing every day. Like them, you can download Processing without cost. You even have the option to modify the Processing code to suit your needs. Processing is a *FLOSS* project (that is, *free/libre/open source software*), and in the spirit of community, we encourage you to participate by sharing your projects and knowledge online at Processing.org and at the many social networking sites that host Processing content (Figure 1-5). These sites are linked from the Processing.org website.

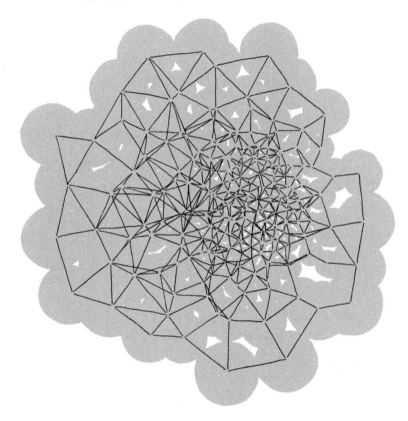

Figure 1-5. Processing is fueled by thousands of people contributing through the Internet. This is our rendition of how they all relate to one another.

2/Starting to Code

To get the most out of this book, you need to do more than just read the words. You need to experiment and practice. You can't learn to code just by reading about it—you need to do it. To get started, download Processing and make your first sketch.

Start by visiting *http://processing.org/download* and selecting the Mac, Windows, or Linux version, depending on what machine you have. Installation on each machine is straightforward:

» On Windows, you'll have a .zip file. Double-click it, and drag the folder inside to a location on your hard disk. It could be *Program Files* or simply the desktop, but the important thing is for the *processing* folder to be pulled out of that .zip file. Then double-click *processing.exe* to start.

» The Mac OS X version is a disk image (.dmg) file. Drag the Processing icon to the *Applications* folder. If you're using someone else's machine and can't modify the *Applications* folder, just drag the application to the desktop. Then double-click the Processing icon to start.

» The Linux version is a .tar.gz file, which should be familiar to most Linux users. Download the file to your home directory, then open a terminal window, and type:

```
tar xvfz processing-xxxx.tgz
```

(Replace xxxx with the rest of the file's name, which is the version number.) This will create a folder named *processing-1.0* or something similar. Then change to that directory:

```
cd processing-xxxx
```

and run it:

```
./processing
```

With any luck, the main Processing window will now be visible (Figure 2-1). Everyone's setup is different, so if the program didn't start, or you're otherwise stuck, visit the troubleshooting page for possible solutions: *http://wiki.processing.org/index.php/Troubleshooting.*

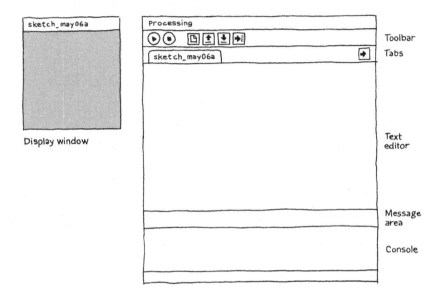

Figure 2-1. The Processing Development Environment.

Your First Program

You're now running the Processing Development Environment (or PDE). There's not much to it; the large area is the Text Editor, and there's a row of buttons across the top; this is the toolbar. Below the editor is the Message Area, and below that is the Console. The Message Area is used for one-line messages, and the Console is used for more technical details.

Example 2-1: Draw an Ellipse

In the editor, type the following:

```
ellipse(50, 50, 80, 80);
```

This line of code means "draw an ellipse, with the center 50 pixels over from the left and 50 pixels down from the top, with a width and height of 80 pixels." Click the Run button, which looks like this:

If you've typed everything correctly, you'll see the ellipse image above. If you didn't type it correctly, the Message Area will turn red and complain about an error. If this happens, make sure that you've copied the example code exactly: the numbers should be contained within parentheses and have commas between each of them, and the line should end with a semicolon.

One of the most difficult things about getting started with programming is that you have to be very specific about the syntax. The Processing software isn't always smart enough to know what you mean, and can be quite fussy about the placement of punctuation. You'll get used to it with a little practice.

Next, we'll skip ahead to a sketch that's a little more exciting.

Example 2-2: Make Circles

Delete the text from the last example, and try this one:

```
void setup() {
  size(480, 120);
  smooth();
}

void draw() {
  if (mousePressed) {
    fill(0);
  } else {
    fill(255);
  }
  ellipse(mouseX, mouseY, 80, 80);
}
```

This program creates a window that is 480 pixels wide and 120 pixels high, and then starts drawing white circles at the position of the mouse. When a mouse button is pressed, the circle color changes to black. We'll explain more about the elements of this program in detail later. For now, run the code, move the mouse, and click to experience it.

Show

So far we've covered only the Run button, though you've probably guessed what the Stop button next to it does:

If you don't want to use the buttons, you can always use the Sketch menu, which reveals the shortcut Ctrl-R (or Cmd-R on the Mac) for Run. Below Run in the Sketch menu is Present, which clears the rest of the screen to present your sketch all by itself:

Sketch	
Run	⌘R
Present	⇧⌘R
Stop	
Import Library...	▶
Show Sketch Folder	⌘K
Add File...	

You can also use Present from the toolbar by holding down the Shift key as you click the Run button.

Save

The next command that's important is Save. It's the downward arrow on the toolbar:

You can also find it under the File menu. By default, your programs are saved to the "sketchbook," which is a folder that collects your programs for easy access. Clicking the Open button on the toolbar (the arrow pointing up) will bring up a list of all the sketches in your sketchbook, as well as a list of examples that are installed with the Processing software:

It's always a good idea to save your sketches often. As you try different things, keep saving with different names, so that you can always go back to an earlier version. This is especially helpful if—no, *when*—something breaks. You can also see where the sketch is located on the disk with Show Sketch Folder under the Sketch menu.

You can also create a new sketch by pressing the New button on the toolbar:

This will replace the sketch in the current window with an empty one. Holding down Shift when you press the New button will create a new sketch in its own window, as will selecting File→New. The Open button works the same way.

Share

Another theme of Processing is sharing your work. The Export button on the toolbar:

will bundle your code into a single folder titled *applet* that can be uploaded to a web server (Figure 2-2). After exporting, the *applet* folder will open on your desktop. The PDE file is the source code, the JAR file is the program, the HTML file is the web page, and the GIF file is displayed in the web browser while the program is loading. Double-clicking the *index.html* file will launch your web browser and show your sketch on the web page it has created.

Applet			
Name	Date Modified	Size	Kind
Ex_02_02.jar	Today	228 KB	Java JAR File
Ex_02_02.java	Today	4 KB	Java Source File
Ex_02_02.pde	Today	4 KB	Processing Source File
index.html	Today	4 KB	HTML Document
loading.gif	10/20/09	4 KB	Graphics Interchange Format (GIF)

Figure 2-2. The applet folder contains the exported sketch.

NOTE: The *applet* folder is erased and recreated each time you use the Export command, so be sure to move the folder elsewhere before you make any changes to the HTML file or anything else inside.

You can also find Export, along with its sibling Export to Application, underneath the File menu. Export to Application creates an application for your choice of Mac, Windows, and/or Linux. This is an easy way to make self-contained, double-clickable versions of your projects (Figure 2-3).

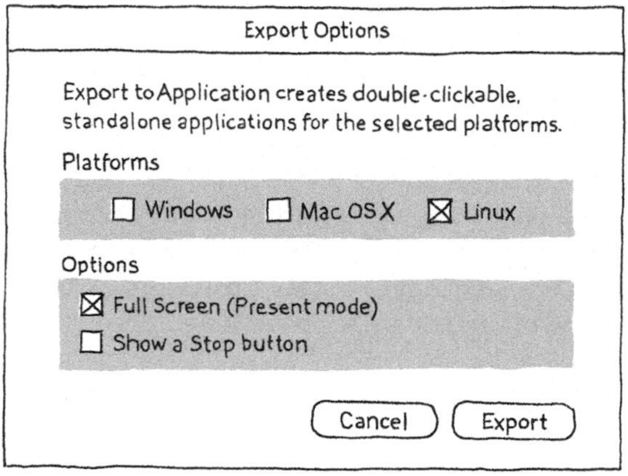

```
┌──────────────────────────────────────────────────┐
│                  Export Options                    │
├──────────────────────────────────────────────────┤
│                                                    │
│  Export to Application creates double-clickable,   │
│  standalone applications for the selected platforms.│
│  Platforms                                         │
│     ☐ Windows    ☐ Mac OS X   ☒ Linux             │
│  Options                                           │
│     ☒ Full Screen (Present mode)                   │
│     ☐ Show a Stop button                           │
│                                                    │
│                    ( Cancel )  ( Export )          │
└──────────────────────────────────────────────────┘
```

Figure 2-3. Export to Application menu.

Holding down Shift when you press the Export button on the toolbar is another way to use Export to Application.

Examples and Reference

Learning how to program with Processing involves exploring lots of code: running, altering, breaking, and enhancing it until you have reshaped it into something new. With this in mind, the Processing software download includes dozens of examples that demonstrate different features of the software. To open an example, select Examples from the File menu or click the Open icon in the PDE. The examples are grouped into categories based on their function, such as Form, Motion, and Image. Find an interesting topic in the list and try an example.

If you see a part of the program you're unfamiliar with that is colored orange (this means it's a part of Processing), select its name, and then click on "Find in Reference" from the Help menu. You can also right-click the text (or Ctrl-click on a Mac) and choose Find in Reference from the menu that appears. This will open the reference for the selected code element in your web browser. The reference is also available online at *http://www.processing.org/reference/*.

The Processing Reference explains every code element with a description and examples. The reference programs are much shorter (usually four or five lines) and easier to follow than the longer code found in the *Examples* folder. We recommend keeping the reference open while you're reading this book and while you're programming. It can be navigated by topic or alphabetically; sometimes it's fastest to do a text search within your browser window.

The reference was written with the beginner in mind; we hope that we've made it clear and understandable. We're grateful to the many people who've spotted errors over the years and reported them. If you think you can improve a reference entry or you find a mistake, please let us know by clicking on the link at the top of each reference page.

3/Draw

At first, drawing on a computer screen is like working on graph paper. It starts as a careful technical procedure, but as new concepts are introduced, drawing simple shapes with software expands into animation and interaction. Before we make this jump, we need to start at the beginning.

A computer screen is a grid of light elements called *pixels*. Each pixel has a position within the grid defined by coordinates. In Processing, the x-coordinate is the distance from the left edge of the Display Window and the y-coordinate is the distance from the top edge. We write coordinates of a pixel like this: (x, y). So, if the screen is 200×200 pixels, the upper-left is (0, 0), the center is at (100, 100), and the lower-right is (199, 199). These numbers may seem confusing; why do we go from 0 to 199 instead of 1 to 200? The answer is that in code, we usually count from 0 because it's easier for calculations that we'll get into later.

The Display Window is created and images are drawn inside through code elements called *functions*. Functions are the basic building blocks of a Processing program. The behavior of a function is defined by its *parameters*. For example, almost every Processing program has a *size()* function to set the width and height of the Display Window. (If your program doesn't have a *size()* function, the dimension is set to 100×100 pixels.)

Example 3-1: Draw a Window

The *size()* function has two parameters: the first sets the width of the window and the second sets the height. To draw a window that is 800 pixels wide and 600 high, write:

```
size(800, 600);
```

Run this line of code to see the result. Put in different values to see what's possible. Try very small numbers and numbers larger than your screen.

Example 3-2: Draw a Point

To set the color of a single pixel within the Display Window, we use the *point()* function. It has two parameters that define a position: the x-coordinate followed by the y-coordinate. To draw a little window and a point at the center of the screen, coordinate (240, 60), type:

```
size(480, 120);
point(240, 60);
```

Try to write a program that puts a point at each corner of the Display Window and one in the center. Try placing points side by side to make horizontal, vertical, and diagonal lines.

Basic Shapes

Processing includes a group of functions to draw basic shapes (see Figure 3-1). Simple shapes like lines can be combined to create more complex forms like a leaf or a face.

To draw a single line, we need four parameters: two for the starting location and two for the end.

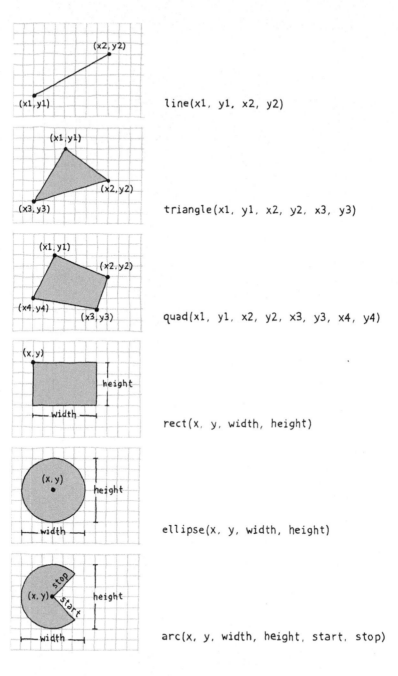

`line(x1, y1, x2, y2)`

`triangle(x1, y1, x2, y2, x3, y3)`

`quad(x1, y1, x2, y2, x3, y3, x4, y4)`

`rect(x, y, width, height)`

`ellipse(x, y, width, height)`

`arc(x, y, width, height, start, stop)`

Figure 3-1. Coordinates and shapes.

Example 3-3: Draw a Line

To draw a line between coordinate (20, 50) and (420,110), try:

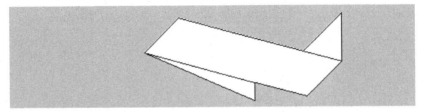

```
size(480, 120);
line(20, 50, 420, 110);
```

Example 3-4: Draw Basic Shapes

Following this pattern, a triangle needs six parameters and a quadrilateral needs eight (one pair for each point):

```
size(480, 120);
quad(158, 55, 199, 14, 392, 66, 351, 107);
triangle(347, 54, 392, 9, 392, 66);
triangle(158, 55, 290, 91, 290, 112);
```

Example 3-5: Draw a Rectangle

Rectangles and ellipses are both defined with four parameters: the first and second are for the x- and y-coordinates of the anchor point, the third for the width, and the fourth for the height. To make a rectangle at coordinate (180, 60) with a width of 220 pixels and height of 40, use the *rect()* function like this:

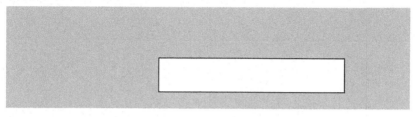

```
size(480, 120);
rect(180, 60, 220, 40);
```

Example 3-6: Draw an Ellipse

The x- and y-coordinates for a rectangle are the upper-left corner, but for an ellipse they are the center of the shape. In this example, notice that the y-coordinate for the first ellipse is outside the window. Objects can be drawn partially (or entirely) out of the window without an error:

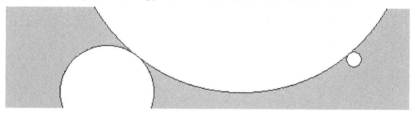

```
size(480, 120);
ellipse(278, -100, 400, 400);
ellipse(120, 100, 110, 110);
ellipse(412, 60, 18, 18);
```

Processing doesn't have separate functions to make squares and circles. To make these shapes, use the same value for the *width* and the *height* parameters to *ellipse()* and *rect()*.

Example 3-7: Draw Part of an Ellipse

The *arc()* function draws a piece of an ellipse:

```
size(480, 120);
arc(90, 60, 80, 80, 0, HALF_PI);
arc(190, 60, 80, 80, 0, PI+HALF_PI);
arc(290, 60, 80, 80, PI, TWO_PI+HALF_PI);
arc(390, 60, 80, 80, QUARTER_PI, PI+QUARTER_PI);
```

The first and second parameters set the location, the third and fourth set the width and height. The fifth parameter sets the angle to start the arc, and the sixth sets the angle to stop. The angles are set in radians, rather than degrees. Radians are angle measurements based on the value of pi (3.14159). Figure 3-2 shows how the two relate. As featured in this example, four radian values are used so frequently that special names for them were added as a part of Processing. The values *PI*, *QUARTER_PI*, *HALF_PI*, and *TWO_PI* can be used to replace the radian values for 180°, 45°, 90°, and 360°.

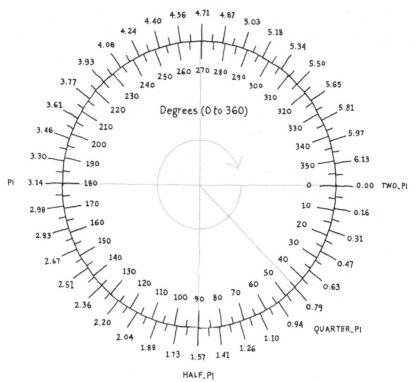

Figure 3-2. Radian and degrees measurements.

Example 3-8: Draw with Degrees

If you prefer to use degree measurements, you can convert to radians
with the *radians()* function. This function takes an angle in degrees and
changes it to the corresponding radian value. The following example is the
same as Example 3-7, but it uses the *radians()* function to define the start
and stop values in degrees:

```
size(480, 120);
arc(90, 60, 80, 80, 0, radians(90));
arc(190, 60, 80, 80, 0, radians(270));
arc(290, 60, 80, 80, radians(180), radians(450));
arc(390, 60, 80, 80, radians(45), radians(225));
```

Drawing Order

When a program runs, the computer starts at the top and reads each line
of code until it reaches the last line and then stops. If you want a shape
to be drawn on top of all other shapes, it needs to follow the others in the
code.

Example 3-9: Control Your Drawing Order

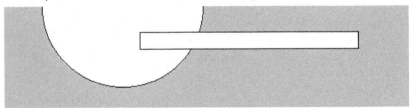

```
size(480, 120);
ellipse(140, 0, 190, 190);
// The rectangle draws on top of the ellipse
// because it comes after in the code
rect(160, 30, 260, 20);
```

Example 3-10: Put It in Reverse

Modify Example 3-9 by reversing the order of *rect()* and *ellipse()* to see the circle on top of the rectangle:

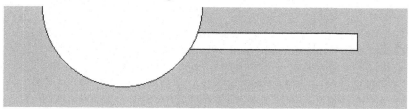

```
size(480, 120);
rect(160, 30, 260, 20);
// The ellipse draws on top of the rectangle
// because it comes after in the code
ellipse(140, 0, 190, 190);
```

You can think of it like painting with a brush or making a collage. The last element that you add is what's visible on top.

Shape Properties

The most basic and useful shape properties are stroke weight and anti-aliasing, also called *smoothing*.

Example 3-11: Draw Smooth Lines

The *smooth()* function smooths the edges of lines drawn to the screen by blending the edges with the nearby pixel values. Conversely, if smoothing is already turned on, the *noSmooth()* function will turn it off:

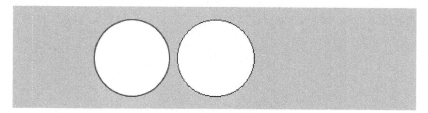

```
size(480, 120);
smooth();  // Turns on smoothing
ellipse(140, 60, 90, 90);
noSmooth();  // Turns off smoothing
ellipse(240, 60, 90, 90);
```

NOTE: Some implementations of Processing (such as the version
for JavaScript) will always smooth shapes; others might not support
smoothing at all. In some situations, it's not possible to enable and disable smoothing within the same trip through *draw()*. See the *smooth()*
reference for more details.

Example 3-12: Set Stroke Weight

The default stroke weight is a single pixel, but this can be changed with
the *strokeWeight()* function. The single parameter to *strokeWeight()* sets
the width of drawn lines:

```
size(480, 120);
smooth();
ellipse(75, 60, 90, 90);
strokeWeight(8);  // Stroke weight to 8 pixels
ellipse(175, 60, 90, 90);
ellipse(279, 60, 90, 90);
strokeWeight(20);  // Stroke weight to 20 pixels
ellipse(389, 60, 90, 90);
```

Example 3-13: Set Stroke Attributes

The *strokeJoin()* function changes the way lines are joined (how the corners look), and the *strokeCap()* function changes how lines are drawn at their beginning and end:

```
size(480, 120);
smooth();
strokeWeight(12);
strokeJoin(ROUND);        // Round the stroke corners
rect(40, 25, 70, 70);
strokeJoin(BEVEL);        // Bevel the stroke corners
rect(140, 25, 70, 70);
strokeCap(SQUARE);        // Square the line endings
line(270, 25, 340, 95);
strokeCap(ROUND);         // Round the line endings
line(350, 25, 420, 95);
```

The placement of shapes like *rect()* and *ellipse()* is controlled with the *rectMode()* and *ellipseMode()* functions. Check the reference (Help→Reference) to see examples of how to place rectangles from their center (rather than their upper-left corner), or to draw ellipses from their upper-left corner like rectangles.

When any of these attributes are set, all shapes drawn afterward are affected. For instance, in Example 3-12, notice how the second and third circles both have the same stroke weight, even though the weight is set only once before both are drawn.

Color

All the shapes so far have been filled white with black outlines, and the background of the Display Window has been light gray. To change them, use the *background()*, *fill()*, and *stroke()* functions. The values of the parameters are in the range of 0 to 255, where 255 is white, 128 is medium gray, and 0 is black. Figure 3-3 shows how the values from 0 to 255 map to different gray levels.

0	64	128	192
1	65	129	193
2	66	130	194
3	67	131	195
4	68	132	196
5	69	133	197
6	70	134	198
7	71	135	199
8	72	136	200
9	73	137	201
10	74	138	202
11	75	139	203
12	76	140	204
13	77	141	205
14	78	142	206
15	79	143	207
16	80	144	208
17	81	145	209
18	82	146	210
19	83	147	211
20	84	148	212
21	85	149	213
22	86	150	214
23	87	151	215
24	88	152	216
25	89	153	217
26	90	154	218
27	91	155	219
28	92	156	220
29	93	157	221
30	94	158	222
31	95	159	223
32	96	160	224
33	97	161	225
34	98	162	226
35	99	163	227
36	100	164	228
37	101	165	229
38	102	166	230
39	103	167	231
40	104	168	232
41	105	169	233
42	106	170	234
43	107	171	235
44	108	172	236
45	109	173	237
46	110	174	238
47	111	175	239
48	112	176	240
49	113	177	241
50	114	178	242
51	115	179	243
52	116	180	244
53	117	181	245
54	118	182	246
55	119	183	247
56	120	184	248
57	121	185	249
58	122	186	250
59	123	187	251
60	124	188	252
61	125	189	253
62	126	190	254
63	127	191	255

Figure 3-3. Gray values from 0 to 255.

Example 3-14: Paint with Grays

This example shows three different gray values on a black background:

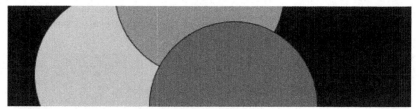

```
size(480, 120);
smooth();
background(0);                       // Black
fill(204);                           // Light gray
ellipse(132, 82, 200, 200);         // Light gray circle
fill(153);                           // Medium gray
ellipse(228, -16, 200, 200);        // Medium gray circle
fill(102);                           // Dark gray
ellipse(268, 118, 200, 200);        // Dark gray circle
```

Example 3-15: Control Fill and Stroke

You can disable the stroke so that there's no outline with *noStroke()* and you can disable the fill of a shape with *noFill()*:

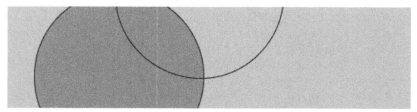

```
size(480, 120);
smooth();
fill(153);                           // Medium gray
ellipse(132, 82, 200, 200);         // Gray circle
noFill();                            // Turn off fill
ellipse(228, -16, 200, 200);        // Outline circle
noStroke();                          // Turn off stroke
ellipse(268, 118, 200, 200);        // Doesn't draw!
```

Be careful not to disable the fill and stroke at the same time, as we've done in the previous example, because nothing will draw to the screen.

Example 3-16: Draw with Color

To move beyond grayscale values, you use three parameters to specify the red, green, and blue components of a color. Because this book is printed in black and white, you'll see only gray value here. Run the code in Processing to reveal the colors:

```
size(480, 120);
noStroke();
smooth();
background(0, 26, 51);        // Dark blue color
fill(255, 0, 0);              // Red color
ellipse(132, 82, 200, 200);   // Red circle
fill(0, 255, 0);              // Green color
ellipse(228, -16, 200, 200);  // Green circle
fill(0, 0, 255);              // Blue color
ellipse(268, 118, 200, 200);  // Blue circle
```

This is referred to as RGB color, which comes from how computers define colors on the screen. The three numbers stand for the values of red, green, and blue, and they range from 0 to 255 the way that the gray values do. Using RGB color isn't very intuitive, so to choose colors, use Tools→Color Selector, which shows a color palette similar to those found in other software (see Figure 3-4). Select a color, and then use the R, G, and B values as the parameters for your *background()*, *fill()*, or *stroke()* function.

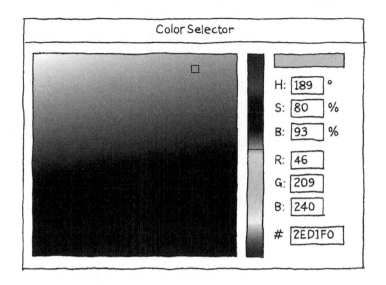

Figure 3-4. Processing Color Selector.

Example 3-17: Set Transparency

By adding an optional fourth parameter to *fill()* or *stroke()*, you can control the transparency. This fourth parameter is known as the *alpha* value, and also uses the range 0 to 255 to set the amount of transparency. The value 0 defines the color as entirely transparent (it won't display), the value 255 is entirely opaque, and the values between these extremes cause the colors to mix on screen:

```
size(480, 120);
noStroke();
smooth();
background(204, 226, 225);      // Light blue color
fill(255, 0, 0, 160);           // Red color
ellipse(132, 82, 200, 200);     // Red circle
fill(0, 255, 0, 160);           // Green color
ellipse(228, -16, 200, 200);    // Green circle
fill(0, 0, 255, 160);           // Blue color
ellipse(268, 118, 200, 200);    // Blue circle
```

Custom Shapes

You're not limited to using these basic geometric shapes—you can also define new shapes by connecting a series of points.

Example 3-18: Draw an Arrow

The *beginShape()* function signals the start of a new shape. The *vertex()* function is used to define each pair of x- and y-coordinates for the shape. Finally, *endShape()* is called to signal that the shape is finished.

```
size(480, 120);
beginShape();
vertex(180, 82);
vertex(207, 36);
vertex(214, 63);
vertex(407, 11);
vertex(412, 30);
vertex(219, 82);
vertex(226, 109);
endShape();
```

Example 3-19: Close the Gap

When you run Example 3-18, you'll see the first and last point are not connected. To do this, add the word *CLOSE* as a parameter to *endShape()*, like this:

```
size(480, 120);
beginShape();
vertex(180, 82);
vertex(207, 36);
vertex(214, 63);
vertex(407, 11);
vertex(412, 30);
vertex(219, 82);
vertex(226, 109);
endShape(CLOSE);
```

Example 3-20: Create Some Creatures

The power of defining shapes with *vertex()* is the ability to make shapes with complex outlines. Processing can draw thousands and thousands of lines at a time to fill the screen with fantastic shapes that spring from your imagination. A modest but more complex example follows:

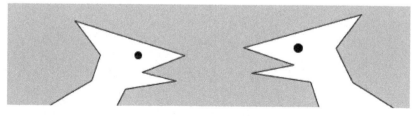

```
size(480, 120);
smooth();

// Left creature
beginShape();
vertex(50, 120);
```

```
vertex(100, 90);
vertex(110, 60);
vertex(80, 20);
vertex(210, 60);
vertex(160, 80);
vertex(200, 90);
vertex(140, 100);
vertex(130, 120);
endShape();
fill(0);
ellipse(155, 60, 8, 8);

// Right creature
fill(255);
beginShape();
vertex(370, 120);
vertex(360, 90);
vertex(290, 80);
vertex(340, 70);
vertex(280, 50);
vertex(420, 10);
vertex(390, 50);
vertex(410, 90);
vertex(460, 120);
endShape();
fill(0);
ellipse(345, 50, 10, 10);
```

Comments

The examples in this chapter use double slashes (//) at the end of a line to add comments to the code. Comments are parts of the program that are ignored when the program is run. They are useful for making notes for yourself that explain what's happening in the code. If others are reading your code, comments are especially important to help them understand your thought process.

Comments are also especially useful for a number of different options, such as when trying to choose the right color. So, for instance, I might be trying to find just the right red for an ellipse:

```
size(200, 200);
fill(165, 57, 57);
ellipse(100, 100, 80, 80);
```

Now suppose I want to try a different red, but don't want to lose the old one. I can copy and paste the line, make a change, and then "comment out" the old one:

```
size(200, 200);
//fill(165, 57, 57);
fill(144, 39, 39);
ellipse(100, 100, 80, 80);
```

Placing // at the beginning of the line temporarily disables it. Or I can remove the // and place it in front of the other line if I want to try it again:

```
size(200, 200);
fill(165, 57, 57);
//fill(144, 39, 39);
ellipse(100, 100, 80, 80);
```

NOTE: As a shortcut, you can also use Ctrl-/ (Cmd-/ on the Mac) to add or remove comments from the current line or a selected block of text. You can also comment out many lines at a time with the alternative comment notation introduced in Appendix A.

As you work with Processing sketches, you'll find yourself creating dozens of iterations of ideas; using comments to make notes or to disable code can help you keep track of multiple options.

Robot 1: Draw

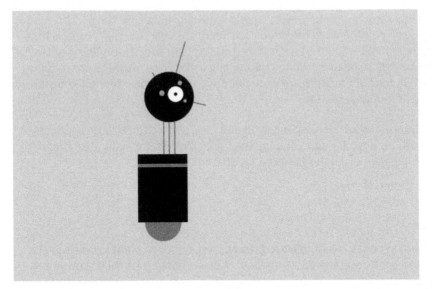

This is P5, the Processing Robot. There are eight different programs to draw and animate him in the book—each one explores a different programming idea. P5's design was inspired by Sputnik I (1957), Shakey from the Stanford Research Institute (1966–1972), the fighter drone in David Lynch's *Dune* (1984), and HAL 9000 from *2001: A Space Odyssey* (1968), among other robot favorites.

The first robot program uses the drawing functions introduced in the previous chapter. The parameters to the *fill()* and *stroke()* functions set the gray values. The *line()*, *ellipse()*, and *rect()* functions define the shapes that create the robot's neck, antennae, body, and head. To get more familiar with the functions, run the program and change the values to redesign the robot:

```
size(720, 480);
smooth();
strokeWeight(2);
background(204);
ellipseMode(RADIUS);

// Neck
stroke(102);                    // Set stroke to gray
line(266, 257, 266, 162);   // Left
line(276, 257, 276, 162);   // Middle
line(286, 257, 286, 162);   // Right

// Antennae
line(276, 155, 246, 112);   // Small
line(276, 155, 306, 56);    // Tall
line(276, 155, 342, 170);   // Medium

// Body
noStroke();                     // Disable stroke
fill(102);                      // Set fill to gray
ellipse(264, 377, 33, 33); // Antigravity orb
fill(0);                        // Set fill to black
rect(219, 257, 90, 120);    // Main body
fill(102);                      // Set fill to gray
rect(219, 274, 90, 6);      // Gray stripe

// Head
fill(0);                        // Set fill to black
ellipse(276, 155, 45, 45); // Head
fill(255);                      // Set fill to white
ellipse(288, 150, 14, 14); // Large eye
fill(0);                        // Set fill to black
ellipse(288, 150, 3, 3);   // Pupil
fill(153);                      // Set fill to light gray
ellipse(263, 148, 5, 5);   // Small eye 1
ellipse(296, 130, 4, 4);   // Small eye 2
ellipse(305, 162, 3, 3);   // Small eye 3
```

4/Variables

A variable stores a value in memory so that it can be used later in a program. The variable can be used many times within a single program, and the value is easily changed while the program is running.

The primary reason we use variables is to avoid repeating ourselves in the code. If you are typing the same number more than once, consider making it into a variable to make your code more general and easier to update.

Example 4-1: Reuse the Same Values

For instance, when you make the y-coordinate and diameter for the two circles in this example into variables, the same values are used for each ellipse:

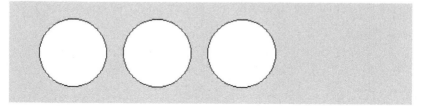

```
size(480, 120);
smooth();
int y = 60;
int d = 80;
ellipse(75, y, d, d);    // Left
ellipse(175, y, d, d);   // Middle
ellipse(275, y, d, d);   // Right
```

Example 4-2: Change Values

Simply changing the *y* and *d* variables therefore alters all three ellipses:

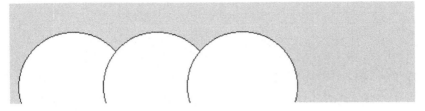

```
size(480, 120);
smooth();
int y = 100;
int d = 130;
ellipse(75, y, d, d);    // Left
ellipse(175, y, d, d);   // Middle
ellipse(275, y, d, d);   // Right
```

Without the variables, you'd need to change the y-coordinate used in the code three times and the diameter six times. When comparing Examples 4-1 and 4-2, notice how the bottom three lines are the same, and only the middle two lines with the variables are different. Variables allow you to separate the lines of the code that change from the lines that don't, which makes programs easier to modify. For instance, if you place variables that control colors and sizes of shapes in one place, then you can quickly explore different visual options by focusing on only a few lines of code.

Making Variables

When you make your own variables, you determine the *name*, the *data type*, and the *value*. The name is what you decide to call the variable. Choose a name that is informative about what the variable stores, but be consistent and not too verbose. For instance, the variable name "radius" will be clearer than "r" when you look at the code later.

The range of values that can be stored within a variable is defined by its *data type*. For instance, the *integer* data type can store numbers without decimal places (whole numbers). In code, *integer* is abbreviated to *int*. There are data types to store each kind of data: integers, floating-point (decimal) numbers, characters, words, images, fonts, and so on.

Variables must first be *declared*, which sets aside space in the computer's memory to store the information. When declaring a variable, you also need to specify its data type (such as *int*), which indicates what kind of information is being stored. After the data type and name are set, a value can be assigned to the variable:

```
int x;    // Declare x as an int variable
x = 12;   // Assign a value to x
```

This code does the same thing, but is shorter:

```
int x = 12; // Declare x as an int variable and assign a value
```

The name of the data type is included on the line of code that declares a variable, but it's not written again. Each time the data type is written in front of the variable name, the computer thinks you're trying to declare a new variable. You can't have two variables with the same name in the same part of the program (see Appendix D), so the program has an error:

```
int x;        // Declare x as an int variable
int x = 12;   // ERROR! Can't have two variables called x here
```

Processing Variables

Processing has a series of special variables to store information about the program while it runs. For instance, the width and height of the window are stored in variables called *width* and *height*. These values are set by the *size()* function. They can be used to draw elements relative to the size of the window, even if the *size()* line changes.

Example 4-3: Adjust the Size, See What Follows

In this example, change the parameters to *size()* to see how it works:

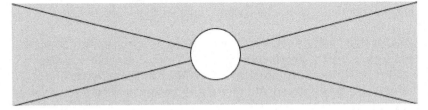

```
size(480, 120);
smooth();
line(0, 0, width, height); // Line from (0,0) to (480, 120)
line(width, 0, 0, height); // Line from (480, 0) to (0, 120)
ellipse(width/2, height/2, 60, 60);
```

Other special variables keep track of the status of the mouse and keyboard values and much more. These are discussed in Chapter 5.

A Little Math

People often assume that math and programming are the same thing. Although knowledge of math can be useful for certain types of coding, basic arithmetic covers the most important parts.

Example 4-4: Basic Arithmetic

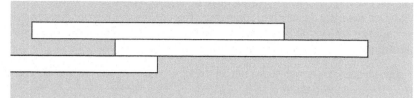

```
size(480, 120);
int x = 25;
int h = 20;
int y = 25;
rect(x, y, 300, h);         // Top
x = x + 100;
rect(x, y + h, 300, h);     // Middle
x = x - 250;
rect(x, y + h*2, 300, h);   // Bottom
```

In code, symbols like +, –, and * are called *operators*. When placed between two values, they create an *expression*. For instance, 5 + 9 and 1024 – 512 are both expressions. The operators for the basic math operations are:

+	Addition
–	Subtraction
*	Multiplication
/	Division
=	Assignment

Processing has a set of rules to define which operators take precedence over others, meaning which calculations are made first, second, third, and so on. These rules define the order in which the code is run. A little knowledge about this goes a long way toward understanding how a short line of code like this works:

```
int x = 4 + 4 * 5;  // Assign 24 to x
```

The expression 4 * 5 is evaluated first because multiplication has the highest priority. Second, 4 is added to the product of 4 * 5 to yield 24. Last, because the assignment operator (the *equal* symbol) has the lowest precedence, the value 24 is assigned to the variable x. This is clarified with parentheses, but the result is the same:

```
int x = 4 + (4 * 5); // Assign 24 to x
```

If you want to force the addition to happen first, just move the parentheses. Because parentheses have a higher precedence than multiplication, the order is changed and the calculation is affected:

```
int x = (4 + 4) * 5; // Assign 40 to x
```

An acronym for this order is often taught in math class: PEMDAS, which stands for Parentheses, Exponents, Multiplication, Division, Addition, Subtraction, where parentheses have the highest priority and subtraction the lowest. The complete order of operations is found in Appendix C.

Some calculations are used so frequently in programming that short-cuts have been developed; it's always nice to save a few keystrokes. For instance, you can add to a variable, or subtract from it, with a single operator:

```
x += 10; // This is the same as x = x + 10
y -= 15; // This is the same as y = y - 15
```

It's also common to add or subtract 1 from a variable, so shortcuts exist for this as well. The ++ and −− operators do this:

```
x++; // This is the same as x = x + 1
y--; // This is the same as y = y - 1
```

More shortcuts can be found in the reference.

Repetition

As you write more programs, you'll notice that patterns occur when lines of code are repeated, but with slight variations. A code structure called a *for* loop makes it possible to run a line of code more than once to condense this type of repetition into fewer lines. This makes your programs more modular and easier to change.

Example 4-5: Do the Same Thing Over and Over

This example has the type of pattern that can be simplified with a *for* loop:

```
size(480, 120);
smooth();
strokeWeight(8);
line(20, 40, 80, 80);
line(80, 40, 140, 80);
line(140, 40, 200, 80);
line(200, 40, 260, 80);
line(260, 40, 320, 80);
line(320, 40, 380, 80);
line(380, 40, 440, 80);
```

Example 4-6: Use a *for* Loop

The same thing can be done with a *for* loop, and with less code:

```
size(480, 120);
smooth();
strokeWeight(8);
for (int i = 20; i < 400; i += 60) {
  line(i, 40, i + 60, 80);
}
```

The *for* loop is different in many ways from the code we've written so far. Notice the braces, the { and } characters. The code between the braces is called a *block*. This is the code that will be repeated on each iteration of the *for* loop.

Inside the parentheses are three statements, separated by semicolons, that work together to control how many times the code inside the block is run. From left to right, these statements are referred to as the *initialization* (*init*), the *test*, and the *update*:

```
for (init; test; update) {
    statements
}
```

The *init* typically declares a new variable to use within the *for* loop and assigns a value. The variable name *i* is frequently used, but there's really nothing special about it. The *test* evaluates the value of this variable, and the *update* changes the variable's value. Figure 4-1 shows the order in which they run and how they control the code statements inside the block.

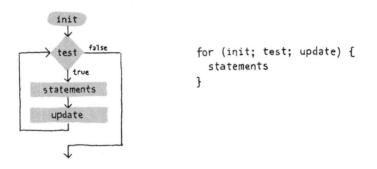

```
for (init; test; update) {
    statements
}
```

Figure 4-1. Flow diagram of a for loop.

The *test* statement requires more explanation. It's always a *relational expression* that compares two values with a *relational operator*. In this example, the expression is "i < 400" and the operator is the < (less than) symbol. The most common relational operators are:

>	Greater than
<	Less than
>=	Greater than or equal to
<=	Less than or equal to
==	Equal to
!=	Not equal to

The relational expression always evaluates to *true* or *false*. For instance, the expression 5 > 3 is *true*. We can ask the question, "Is five greater than three?" Because the answer is "yes," we say the expression is *true*.

For the expression 5 < 3, we ask, "Is five less than three?" Because the answer is "no," we say the expression is *false*. When the evaluation is *true*, the code inside the block is run, and when it's *false*, the code inside the block is not run and the *for* loop ends.

Example 4-7: Flex Your *for* Loop's Muscles

The ultimate power of working with a *for* loop is the ability to make quick changes to the code. Because the code inside the block is typically run multiple times, a change to the block is magnified when the code is run. By modifying Example 4-6 only slightly, we can create a range of different patterns:

```
size(480, 120);
smooth();
strokeWeight(2);
for (int i = 20; i < 400; i += 8) {
  line(i, 40, i + 60, 80);
}
```

Example 4-8: Fanning Out the Lines

```
size(480, 120);
smooth();
strokeWeight(2);
for (int i = 20; i < 400; i += 20) {
  line(i, 0, i + i/2, 80);
}
```

Example 4-9: Kinking the Lines

```
size(480, 120);
smooth();
strokeWeight(2);
for (int i = 20; i < 400; i += 20) {
  line(i, 0, i + i/2, 80);
  line(i + i/2, 80, i*1.2, 120);
}
```

Example 4-10: Embed One *for* Loop in Another

When one *for* loop is embedded inside another, the number of repetitions is multiplied. First, let's look at a short example, and then we'll break it down in Example 4-11:

```
size(480, 120);
background(0);
smooth();
noStroke();
for (int y = 0; y <= height; y += 40) {
  for (int x = 0; x <= width; x += 40) {
    fill(255, 140);
    ellipse(x, y, 40, 40);
  }
}
```

Example 4-11: Rows and Columns

In this example, the *for* loops are adjacent, rather than one embedded inside the other. The result shows that one *for* loop is drawing a column of 4 circles and the other is drawing a row of 13 circles:

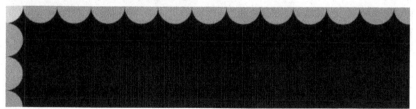

```
size(480, 120);
background(0);
smooth();
noStroke();
for (int y = 0; y < height+45; y += 40) {
  fill(255, 140);
  ellipse(0, y, 40, 40);
}
for (int x = 0; x < width+45; x += 40) {
  fill(255, 140);
  ellipse(x, 0, 40, 40);
}
```

When one of these *for* loops is placed inside the other, as in Example 4-10, the 4 repetitions of the first loop are compounded with the 13 of the second in order to run the code inside the embedded block 52 times (4×13 = 52).

Example 4-10 is a good base for exploring many types of repeating visual patterns. The following examples show a couple of ways that it can be extended, but this is only a tiny sample of what's possible. In Example 4-12, the code draws a line from each point in the grid to the center of the screen. In Example 4-13, the ellipses shrink with each new row and are moved to the right by adding the y-coordinate to the x-coordinate.

Example 4-12: Pins and Lines

```
size(480, 120);
background(0);
smooth();
fill(255);
stroke(102);
for (int y = 20; y <= height-20; y += 10) {
  for (int x = 20; x <= width-20; x += 10) {
    ellipse(x, y, 4, 4);
    // Draw a line to the center of the display
    line(x, y, 240, 60);
  }
}
```

Example 4-13: Halftone Dots

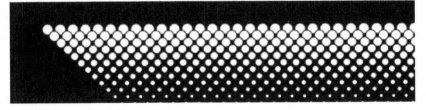

```
size(480, 120);
background(0);
smooth();
for (int y = 32; y <= height; y += 8) {
  for (int x = 12; x <= width; x += 15) {
    ellipse(x + y, y, 16 - y/10.0, 16 - y/10.0);
  }
}
```

Robot 2: Variables

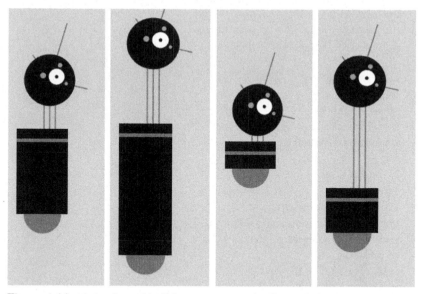

The variables introduced in this program make the code look more difficult than Robot 1 (see "Robot 1: Draw" in Chapter 3), but now it's much easier to modify, because numbers that depend on one another are in a single location. For instance, the neck can be drawn based on the *body-Height* variable. The group of variables at the top of the code control the aspects of the robot that we want to change: location, body height, and neck height. You can see some of the range of possible variations in the figure; from left to right, here are the values that correspond to them:

```
y = 390              y = 460              y = 310              y = 420
bodyHeight = 180     bodyHeight = 260     bodyHeight = 80      bodyHeight = 110
neckHeight = 40      neckHeight = 95      neckHeight = 10      neckHeight = 140
```

When altering your own code to use variables instead of numbers, plan the changes carefully, then make the modifications in short steps. For instance, when this program was written, each variable was created one at a time to minimize the complexity of the transition. After a variable was added and the code was run to ensure it was working, the next variable was added:

```
int x = 60;              // x-coordinate
int y = 420;             // y-coordinate
int bodyHeight = 110;    // Body Height
int neckHeight = 140;    // Neck Height
int radius = 45;         // Head Radius
int ny = y - bodyHeight - neckHeight - radius;  // Neck Y

size(170, 480);
smooth();
strokeWeight(2);
background(204);
ellipseMode(RADIUS);

// Neck
stroke(102);
line(x+2, y-bodyHeight, x+2, ny);
line(x+12, y-bodyHeight, x+12, ny);
line(x+22, y-bodyHeight, x+22, ny);
// Antennae
line(x+12, ny, x-18, ny-43);
line(x+12, ny, x+42, ny-99);
line(x+12, ny, x+78, ny+15);
// Body
noStroke();
fill(102);
ellipse(x, y-33, 33, 33);
fill(0);
rect(x-45, y-bodyHeight, 90, bodyHeight-33);
fill(102);
rect(x-45, y-bodyHeight+17, 90, 6);
// Head
fill(0);
ellipse(x+12, ny, radius, radius);
fill(255);
ellipse(x+24, ny-6, 14, 14);
fill(0);
ellipse(x+24, ny-6, 3, 3);
fill(153);
ellipse(x, ny-8, 5, 5);
ellipse(x+30, ny-26, 4, 4);
ellipse(x+41, ny+6, 3, 3);
```

5/Response

Code that responds to input from the mouse, keyboard, and other devices has to run continuously. To make this happen, place the lines that update inside a Processing function called *draw()*.

Example 5-1: The *draw()* Function

To see how *draw()* works, run this example:

```
void draw() {
  // Displays the frame count to the Console
  println("I'm drawing");
  println(frameCount);
}
```

You'll see the following:

```
I'm drawing
1
I'm drawing
2
I'm drawing
3
...
```

The code within the *draw()* block runs from top to bottom, then repeats until you quit the program by clicking the Stop button or closing the window. Each trip through *draw()* is called a *frame*. (The default frame rate is 60 frames per second, but this can be changed. See Example 7-2 for more information.) In the previous example program, the *println()* functions write the text "I'm drawing" followed by the current frame count as counted by the special *frameCount* variable (1, 2, 3, ...). The text appears in the Console, the black area at the bottom of the Processing editor window.

Example 5-2: The *setup()* Function

To complement the looping *draw()* function, Processing has a function called *setup()* that runs just once when the program starts:

```
void setup() {
  println("I'm starting");
}

void draw() {
  println("I'm running");
}
```

When this code is run, the following is written to the Console:

```
I'm starting
I'm running
I'm running
I'm running
...
```

The text "I'm running" continues to write to the Console until the program is stopped.

In a typical program, the code inside *setup()* is used to define the starting values. The first line is always the *size()* function, often followed by code to set the starting fill and stroke colors, or perhaps to load images and fonts. (If you don't include the *size()* function, the Display Window will be 100×100 pixels.)

Now you know how to use *setup()* and *draw()*, but this isn't the whole story. There's one more location to put code—you can also place variables outside of *setup()* and *draw()*. If you create a variable inside of *setup()*, you can't use it inside of *draw()*, so you need to place those variables somewhere else. Such variables are called *global* variables, because they can be used anywhere ("globally") in the program. This is clearer when we list the order in which the code is run:

1. Variables declared outside of *setup()* and *draw()* are created.

2. Code inside *setup()* is run once.

3. Code inside *draw()* is run continuously.

Example 5-3: *setup()*, Meet *draw()*

The following example puts it all together:

```
int x = 280;
int y = -100;
int diameter = 380;

void setup() {
  size(480, 120);
  smooth();
  fill(102);
}

void draw() {
  background(204);
  ellipse(x, y, diameter, diameter);
}
```

Follow

Now that we have code running continuously, we can track the mouse position and use those numbers to move elements on screen.

Example 5-4: Track the Mouse

The *mouseX* variable stores the x-coordinate, and the *mouseY* variable stores the y-coordinate:

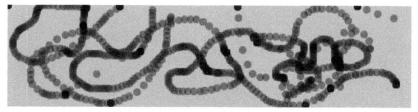

```
void setup() {
  size(480, 120);
  fill(0, 102);
  smooth();
  noStroke();
}
```

```
void draw() {
  ellipse(mouseX, mouseY, 9, 9);
}
```

In this example, each time the code in the *draw()* block is run, a new circle is drawn to the window. This image was made by moving the mouse around to control the circle's location. Because the fill is set to be partially transparent, denser black areas show where the mouse spent more time and where it moved slowly. The circles that are spaced farther apart show when the mouse was moving faster.

Example 5-5: The Dot Follows You

In this example, a new circle is added to the window each time the code in *draw()* is run. To refresh the screen and only display the newest circle, place a *background()* function at the beginning of *draw()* before the shape is drawn:

```
void setup() {
  size(480, 120);
  fill(0, 102);
  smooth();
  noStroke();
}

void draw() {
  background(204);
  ellipse(mouseX, mouseY, 9, 9);
}
```

The *background()* function clears the entire window, so be sure to always place it before other functions inside *draw()*; otherwise, the shapes drawn before it will be erased.

Example 5-6: Draw Continuously

The *pmouseX* and *pmouseY* variables store the position of the r...
the previous frame. Like *mouseX* and *mouseY*, these special variables are
updated each time *draw()* runs. When combined, they can be used to
draw continuous lines by connecting the current and most recent
location:

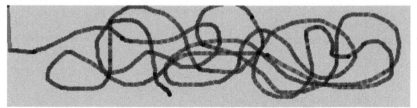

```
void setup() {
  size(480, 120);
  strokeWeight(4);
  smooth();
  stroke(0, 102);
}

void draw() {
  line(mouseX, mouseY, pmouseX, pmouseY);
}
```

Example 5-7: Set Thickness on the Fly

The *pmouseX* and *pmouseY* variables can also be used to calculate the
speed of the mouse. This is done by measuring the distance between the
current and most recent mouse location. If the mouse is moving slowly,
the distance is small, but if the mouse starts moving faster, the distance
grows. A function called *dist()* simplifies this calculation, as shown in the
following example. Here, the speed of the mouse is used to set the
thickness of the drawn line:

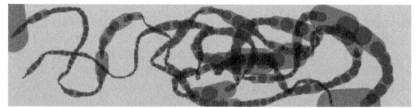

```
void setup() {
  size(480, 120);
  smooth();
  stroke(0, 102);
}

void draw() {
  float weight = dist(mouseX, mouseY, pmouseX, pmouseY);
  strokeWeight(weight);
  line(mouseX, mouseY, pmouseX, pmouseY);
}
```

Example 5-8: Easing Does It

In Example 5-7, the values from the mouse are converted directly into
positions on the screen. But sometimes you want the values to follow the
mouse loosely—to lag behind to create a more fluid motion. This technique is called *easing*. With easing, there are two values: the current value
and the value to move toward (see Figure 5-1). At each step in the program, the current value moves a little closer to the target value:

```
float x;
float easing = 0.01;

void setup() {
  size(220, 120);
  smooth();
}

void draw() {
  float targetX = mouseX;
  x += (targetX - x) * easing;
  ellipse(x, 40, 12, 12);
  println(targetX + " : " + x);
}
```

The value of the *x* variable is always getting closer to *targetX*. The speed at
which it catches up with *targetX* is set with the *easing* variable, a number between 0 and 1. A small value for easing causes more of a delay than a larger
value. With an easing value of 1, there is no delay. When you run Example
5-8, the actual values are shown in the Console through the *println()* function. When moving the mouse, notice how the numbers are far apart, but
when the mouse stops moving, the *x* value gets closer to *targetX*.

easing = 0.1

• • • • • • • • • • • • • • •••••••••••••••••●

Start   Target

easing = 0.2

•   •   •   •   •   •   • • •••••••●

Start   Target

easing = 0.3

•   •   •   •   •   • • ••●

Start   Target

easing = 0.4

•   •   •   •   • ••●

Start   Target

Figure 5-1. Easing.

All of the work in this example happens on the line that begins x +=.
There, the difference between the target and current value is calculated,
then multiplied by the easing variable and added to x to bring it closer to
the target.

Example 5-9: Smooth Lines with Easing

In this example, the easing technique is applied to Example 5-7. In comparison, the lines are smoother:

```
float x;
float y;
```

```
float px;
float py;
float easing = 0.05;

void setup() {
  size(480, 120);
  smooth();
  stroke(0, 102);
}

void draw() {
  float targetX = mouseX;
  x += (targetX - x) * easing;
  float targetY = mouseY;
  y += (targetY - y) * easing;
  float weight = dist(x, y, px, py);
  strokeWeight(weight);
  line(x, y, px, py);
  py = y;
  px = x;
}
```

Map

When numbers are used to draw to the screen, it's often useful to convert the values from one range of numbers to another.

Example 5-10: Map Values to a Range

The *mouseX* variable is usually between 0 and the width of the window, but you might want to remap those values to a different range of coordinates. You can do this by making calculations like dividing *mouseX* by a number to reduce its range and then adding or subtracting a number to shift it left or right:

```
void setup() {
  size(240, 120);
  strokeWeight(12);
  smooth();
}

void draw() {
  background(204);
  stroke(255);
  line(120, 60, mouseX, mouseY);   // White line
  stroke(0);
  float mx = mouseX/2 + 60;
  line(120, 60, mx, mouseY);   // Black line
}
```

The *map()* function is a more general way to make this type of change. It converts a variable from one range of numbers to another. The first parameter is the variable to be converted, the second and third parameters are the low and high values of that variable, and the fourth and fifth parameters are the desired low and high values. The *map()* function hides the math behind the conversion.

Example 5-11: Map with the *map()* Function

This example rewrites Example 5-10 using *map()*:

```
void setup() {
  size(240, 120);
  strokeWeight(12);
  smooth();
}

void draw() {
  background(204);
  stroke(255);
  line(120, 60, mouseX, mouseY);   // White line
  stroke(0);
  float mx = map(mouseX, 0, width, 60, 180);
  line(120, 60, mx, mouseY);   // Black line
}
```

The *map()* function makes the code easy to read, because the minimum and maximum values are clearly written as the parameters. In this example, *mouseX* values between 0 and *width* are converted to a number from

60 (when *mouseX* is 0) up to 180 (when *mouseX* is *width*). You'll find the useful *map()* function in many examples throughout this book.

Click

In addition to the location of the mouse, Processing also keeps track of whether the mouse button is pressed. The *mousePressed* variable has a different value when the mouse button is pressed and when it is not. The *mousePressed* variable is a data type called *boolean*, which means that it has only two possible values: *true* and *false*. The value of *mousePressed* is *true* when a button is pressed.

Example 5-12: Click the Mouse

The *mousePressed* variable is used along with the *if* statement to determine when a line of code will run and when it won't. Try this example before we explain further:

```
void setup() {
  size(240, 120);
  smooth();
  strokeWeight(30);
}

void draw() {
  background(204);
  stroke(102);
  line(40, 0, 70, height);
  if (mousePressed == true) {
    stroke(0);
  }
  line(0, 70, width, 50);
}
```

In this program, the code inside the *if* block runs only when a mouse button is pressed. When a button is not pressed, this code is ignored. Like the *for* loop discussed in "Repetition" in Chapter 4, the *if* also has a *test* that is evaluated to *true* or *false*:

```
if (test) {
  statements
}
```

When the test is *true*, the code inside the block is run; when the test is *false*, the code inside the block is not run. The computer determines whether the test is *true* or *false* by evaluating the expression inside the parentheses. (If you'd like to refresh your memory, the discussion of relational expressions is with Example 4-6.)

The == symbol compares the values on the left and right to test whether they are equivalent. This == symbol is different from the assignment operator, the single = symbol. The == symbol asks, "Are these things equal?" and the = symbol sets the value of a variable.

NOTE: It's a common mistake, even for experienced programmers, to write = in your code when you mean to write ==. The Processing software won't always warn you when you do this, so be careful.

Alternatively, the test in *draw()* in Example 5-12 can be written like this:

```
if (mousePressed) {
```

Boolean variables, including *mousePressed*, don't need the explicit comparison with the == operator, because they can be only *true* or *false*.

Example 5-13: Detect When Not Clicked

A single *if* block gives you the choice of running some code or skipping it.
You can extend an *if* block with an *else* block, allowing your program to
choose between two options. The code inside the *else* block runs when
the value of the *if* block test is *false*. For instance, the stroke color for a
program can be white when the mouse button is not pressed, and can
change to black when the button is pressed:

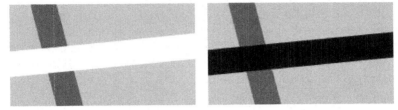

```
void setup() {
  size(240, 120);
  smooth();
  strokeWeight(30);
}

void draw() {
  background(204);
  stroke(102);
  line(40, 0, 70, height);
  if (mousePressed) {
    stroke(0);
  } else {
    stroke(255);
  }
  line(0, 70, width, 50);
}
```

Example 5-14: Multiple Mouse Buttons

Processing also tracks which button is pressed if you have more than one button on your mouse. The *mouseButton* variable can be one of three values: *LEFT, CENTER,* or *RIGHT.* To test which button was pressed, the == operator is needed, as shown here:

```
void setup() {
  size(120, 120);
  smooth();
  strokeWeight(30);
}

void draw() {
  background(204);
  stroke(102);
  line(40, 0, 70, height);
  if (mousePressed) {
    if (mouseButton == LEFT) {
      stroke(255);
    } else {
      stroke(0);
    }
    line(0, 70, width, 50);
  }
}
```

A program can have many more *if* and *else* structures (see Figure 5-2) than those found in these short examples. They can be chained together into a long series with each testing for something different, and *if* blocks can be embedded inside of other *if* blocks to make more complex decisions.

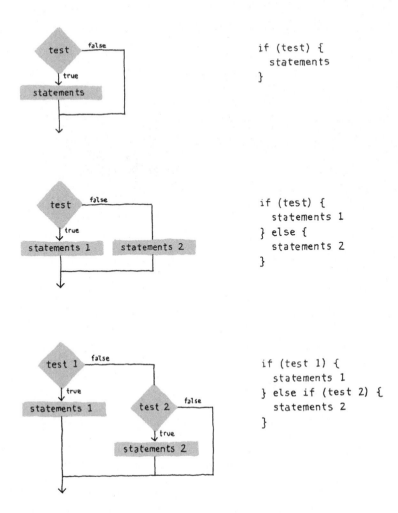

```
if (test) {
    statements
}
```

```
if (test) {
    statements 1
} else {
    statements 2
}
```

```
if (test 1) {
    statements 1
} else if (test 2) {
    statements 2
}
```

Figure 5-2. The if and else structure makes decisions about which blocks of code to run.

Location

An if structure can be used with the mouseX and mouseY values to determine the location of the cursor within the window.

Example 5-15: Find the Cursor

For instance, this example tests to see whether the cursor is on the left or right side of a line and then moves the line toward the cursor:

```
float x;
int offset = 10;

void setup() {
  size(240, 120);
  smooth();
  x = width/2;
}

void draw() {
  background(204);
  if (mouseX > x) {
    x += 0.5;
    offset = -10;
  }
  if (mouseX < x) {
    x -= 0.5;
    offset = 10;
  }
  line(x, 0, x, height);
  line(mouseX, mouseY, mouseX + offset, mouseY - 10);
  line(mouseX, mouseY, mouseX + offset, mouseY + 10);
  line(mouseX, mouseY, mouseX + offset*3, mouseY);
}
```

To write programs that have graphical user interfaces (buttons, check-boxes, scrollbars, and so on), we need to write code that knows when the cursor is within an enclosed area of the screen. The following two examples introduce how to check whether the cursor is inside a circle and a rectangle. The code is written in a modular way with variables, so it can be used to check for *any* circle and rectangle by changing the values.

Example 5-16: The Bounds of a Circle

For the circle test, we use the *dist()* function to get the distance from the center of the circle to the cursor, then we test to see if that distance is less than the radius of the circle (see Figure 5-3). If it is, we know we're inside. In this example, when the cursor is within the area of the circle, its size increases:

```
int x = 120;
int y = 60;
int radius = 12;

void setup() {
  size(240, 120);
  smooth();
  ellipseMode(RADIUS);
}

void draw() {
  background(204);
  float d = dist(mouseX, mouseY, x, y);
  if (d < radius) {
    radius++;
    fill(0);
  } else {
    fill(255);
  }
  ellipse(x, y, radius, radius);
}
```

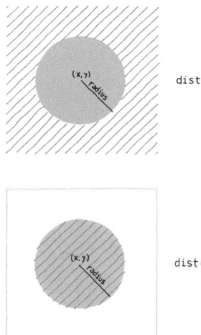

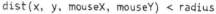

dist(x, y, mouseX, mouseY) > radius

dist(x, y, mouseX, mouseY) < radius

Figure 5-3. Circle rollover test.

Example 5-17: The Bounds of a Rectangle

We use another approach to test whether the cursor is inside a rectangle. We make four separate tests to check if the cursor is on the correct side of each edge of the rectangle, then we compare each test and if they are all *true*, we know the cursor is inside. This is illustrated in Figure 5-4. Each step is simple, but it looks complicated when it's all put together:

```
int x = 80;
int y = 30;
int w = 80;
int h = 60;

void setup() {
  size(240, 120);
}

void draw() {
  background(204);
  if ((mouseX > x) && (mouseX < x+w) &&
      (mouseY > y) && (mouseY < y+h)) {
    fill(0);
  } else {
    fill(255);
  }
  rect(x, y, w, h);
}
```

The test in the *if* statement is a little more complicated than we've seen. Four individual tests (e.g., *mouseX > x*) are combined with the logical AND operator, the *&&* symbol, to ensure that every relational expression in the sequence is *true*. If one of them is *false*, the entire test is *false* and the fill color won't be set to black. This is explained further in the reference entry for *&&*.

Type

Processing keeps track of when any key on a keyboard is pressed, as well as the last key pressed. Like the *mousePressed* variable, the *keyPressed* variable is *true* when any key is pressed, and *false* when no keys are pressed.

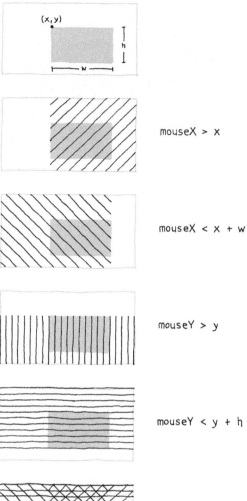

Figure 5-4. Rectangle rollover test.

Example 5-18: Tap a Key

In this example, the second line is drawn only when a key is pressed:

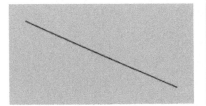 

```
void setup() {
  size(240, 120);
  smooth();
}

void draw() {
  background(204);
  line(20, 20, 220, 100);
  if (keyPressed) {
    line(220, 20, 20, 100);
  }
}
```

The *key* variable stores the most recent key that has been pressed. The data type for *key* is *char*, which is short for "character" but usually pronounced like the first syllable of "charcoal." A *char* variable can store any single character, which includes letters of the alphabet, numbers, and symbols. Unlike a *string* value (see Example 6-8), which is distinguished by double quotes, the *char* data type is specified by single quotes. This is how a *char* variable is declared and assigned:

```
char c = 'A';  // Declares and assigns 'A' to the variable c
```

And these attempts will cause an error:

```
char c = "A";  // Error! Can't assign a String to a char
char h = A;    // Error! Missing the single quotes from 'A'
```

Unlike the *boolean* variable *keyPressed*, which reverts to *false* each time a key is released, the *key* variable keeps its value until the next key is pressed. The following example uses the value of *key* to draw the character to the screen. Each time a new key is pressed, the value updates and a new character draws. Some keys, like Shift and Alt, don't have a visible character, so when you press them, nothing is drawn.

Example 5-19: Draw Some Letters

This example introduces the *textSize()* function to set the size of the letters, the *textAlign()* function to center the text on its x-coordinate, and the *text()* function to draw the letter. These functions are discussed in more detail on pages 84–85.

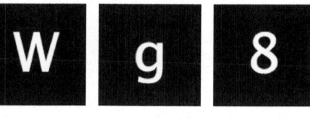

```
void setup() {
  size(120, 120);
  textSize(64);
  textAlign(CENTER);
}

void draw() {
  background(0);
  text(key, 60, 80);
}
```

By using an *if* structure, we can test to see whether a specific key is pressed and choose to draw something on screen in response.

Example 5-20: Check for Specific Keys

In this example, we test for an H or N to be typed. We use the comparison operator, the == symbol, to see if the *key* value is equal to the characters we're looking for:

```
void setup() {
  size(120, 120);
  smooth();
}

void draw() {
  background(204);
  if (keyPressed) {
    if ((key == 'h') || (key == 'H')) {
      line(30, 60, 90, 60);
    }
    if ((key == 'n') || (key == 'N')) {
      line(30, 20, 90, 100);
    }
  }
  line(30, 20, 30, 100);
  line(90, 20, 90, 100);
}
```

When we watch for H or N to be pressed, we need to check for both the lowercase and uppercase letters in the event that someone hits the Shift key or has the Caps Lock set. We combine the two tests together with a logical OR, the || symbol. If we translate the second *if* statement in this example into plain language, it says, "If the 'h' key is pressed OR the 'H' key is pressed." Unlike Example 5-17 with the logical AND (the && symbol), only one of these expressions need be *true* for the entire *test* to be *true*.

Some keys are more difficult to detect, because they aren't tied to a particular letter. Keys like Shift, Alt, and the arrow keys are *coded* and require an extra step to figure out if they are pressed. First, we need to check if the key that's been pressed is a coded key, then we check the code with the *keyCode* variable to see which key it is. The most frequently used *keyCode* values are *ALT*, *CONTROL*, and *SHIFT*, as well as the arrow keys, *UP*, *DOWN*, *LEFT*, and *RIGHT*.

Example 5-21: Move with Arrow Keys

The following example shows how to check for the left or right arrow keys to move a rectangle:

```
int x = 215;

void setup() {
  size(480, 120);
}

void draw() {
  if (keyPressed && (key == CODED)) {  // If it's a coded key
    if (keyCode == LEFT) {             // If it's the left arrow
      x--;
    } else if (keyCode == RIGHT) {     // If it's the right arrow
      x++;
    }
  }
  rect(x, 45, 50, 50);
}
```

Robot 3: Response

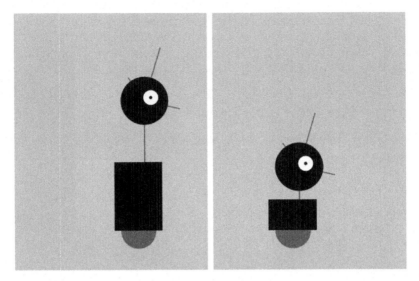

This program uses the variables introduced in Robot 2 (see "Robot 2: Variables" in Chapter 4) and makes it possible to change them while the program runs so that the shapes respond to the mouse. The code inside the *draw()* block runs many times each second. At each frame, the variables defined in the program change in response to the *mouseX* and *mousePressed* variables.

The *mouseX* value controls the position of the robot with an easing technique so that movements are less instantaneous and therefore feel more natural. When a mouse button is pressed, the values of *neckHeight* and *bodyHeight* change to make the robot short.

```
float x = 60;            // X-coordinate
float y = 440;           // Y-coordinate
int radius = 45;         // Head Radius
int bodyHeight = 160;    // Body Height
int neckHeight = 70;     // Neck Height

float easing = 0.02;

void setup() {
  size(360, 480);
  smooth();
  strokeWeight(2);
```

```
    ellipseMode(RADIUS);
}

void draw() {

  int targetX = mouseX;
  x += (targetX - x) * easing;

  if (mousePressed) {
    neckHeight = 16;
    bodyHeight = 90;
  } else {
    neckHeight = 70;
    bodyHeight = 160;
  }

  float ny = y - bodyHeight - neckHeight - radius;

  background(204);

  // Neck
  stroke(102);
  line(x+12, y-bodyHeight, x+12, ny);

  // Antennae
  line(x+12, ny, x-18, ny-43);
  line(x+12, ny, x+42, ny-99);
  line(x+12, ny, x+78, ny+15);

  // Body
  noStroke();
  fill(102);
  ellipse(x, y-33, 33, 33);
  fill(0);
  rect(x-45, y-bodyHeight, 90, bodyHeight-33);

  // Head
  fill(0);
  ellipse(x+12, ny, radius, radius);
  fill(255);
  ellipse(x+24, ny-6, 14, 14);
  fill(0);
  ellipse(x+24, ny-6, 3, 3);
}
```

6/Media

Processing is capable of drawing more than simple lines and shapes. It's time to learn how to load raster images, vector files, and fonts into our programs to extend the visual possibilities to photography, detailed diagrams, and diverse typefaces.

Processing uses a folder named *data* to store such files, so that you never have to think about their location when making a sketch that will run on the desktop, on the Web, or on a mobile device. We've posted some media files online for you to use in this chapter's examples: *http://www.processing.org/learning/books/media.zip*.

Download this file, unzip it to the desktop (or somewhere else convenient), and make a mental note of its location.

NOTE: To unzip on Mac OS X, just double-click the file, and it will create a folder named *media*. On Windows, double-click the *media.zip* file, which will open a new window. In that window, drag the *media* folder to the desktop.

Create a new sketch, and select Add File from the Sketch menu. Find the *lunar.jpg* file from the media folder that you just unzipped and select it. If everything went well, the message area will read "1 file added to the sketch."

To check for the file, select Show Sketch Folder in the Sketch menu. You should see a folder named *data*, with a copy of *lunar.jpg* inside. When you add a file to the sketch, the *data* folder will automatically be created. Instead of using the Add File menu command, you can do the same thing by dragging files into the editor area of the Processing window. The files will be copied to the *data* folder the same way (and the *data* folder will be created if none exists).

You can also create the *data* folder outside of Processing and copy files there yourself. You won't get the message saying that files have been added, but this is a helpful method when you're working with large numbers of files.

NOTE: On Windows and Mac OS X, extensions are hidden by default. It's a good idea to change that option so that you always see the full name of your files. On Mac OS X, select Preferences from the Finder menu, and then make sure "Show all filename extensions" is checked in the Advanced tab. On Windows, look for "Folder Options," and set the option there.

Images

There are three steps to follow before you can draw an image to the screen:

1. Add the image to the sketch's *data* folder (instructions given previously).

2. Create a *PImage* variable to store the image.

3. Load the image into the variable with *loadImage()*.

Example 6-1: Load an Image

After all three steps are done, you can draw the image to the screen with the *image()* function. The first parameter to *image()* specifies the image to draw; the second and third set the x- and y-coordinates:

```
PImage img;

void setup() {
  size(480, 120);
  img = loadImage("lunar.jpg");
}

void draw() {
  image(img, 0, 0);
}
```

Optional fourth and fifth parameters set the width and height to draw the image. If the fourth and fifth parameters are not used, the image is drawn at the size at which it was created.

These next examples show how to work with more than one image in the same program and how to resize an image.

Example 6-2: Load More Images

For this example, you'll need to add the *capsule.jpg* file (found in the *media* folder you downloaded) to your sketch using one of the methods described earlier.

```
PImage img1;
PImage img2;

void setup() {
  size(480, 120);
  img1 = loadImage("lunar.jpg");
  img2 = loadImage("capsule.jpg");
}

void draw() {
  image(img1, -120, 0);
  image(img1, 130, 0, 240, 120);
  image(img2, 300, 0, 240, 120);
}
```

Example 6-3: Mousing Around with Images

When the *mouseX* and *mouseY* values are used as part of the fourth and fifth parameters of *image()*, the image size changes as the mouse moves:

```
PImage img;

void setup() {
  size(480, 120);
  img = loadImage("lunar.jpg");
}

void draw() {
  background(0);
  image(img, 0, 0, mouseX * 2, mouseY * 2);
}
```

NOTE: When an image is displayed larger or smaller than its actual size, it may become distorted. Be careful to prepare your images at the sizes they will be used. When the display size of an image is changed with the *image()* function, the actual image on the hard drive doesn't change.

Processing can load and display raster images in the JPEG, PNG, and GIF formats. (Vector shapes in the SVG format can be displayed in a different way, as described in "Shapes," later in this chapter.) You can convert images to the JPEG, PNG, and GIF formats using programs like GIMP and Photoshop. Most digital cameras save JPEG images, but they usually need to be reduced in size before being used with Processing. A typical digital camera creates an image that is several times larger than the drawing area of most Processing sketches, so resizing such images before they are added to the *data* folder makes sketches run more efficiently, and can save disk space.

GIF and PNG images support transparency, which means that pixels can be invisible or partially visible (recall the discussion of *color()* and alpha values on pages 26–29). GIF images have 1-bit transparency, which means that pixels are either fully opaque or fully transparent. PNG images have 8-bit transparency, which means that each pixel can have a variable level of opacity. The following examples show the difference, using the *clouds. gif* and *clouds.png* files found in the *media* folder that you downloaded. Be sure to add them to the sketch before trying each example.

Example 6-4: Transparency with a GIF

```
PImage img;

void setup() {
  size(480, 120);
  img = loadImage("clouds.gif");
}
void draw() {
  background(255);
  image(img, 0, 0);
  image(img, 0, mouseY * -1);
}
```

Example 6-5: Transparency with a PNG

```
PImage img;

void setup() {
  size(480, 120);
  img = loadImage("clouds.png");
}

void draw() {
  background(204);
  image(img, 0, 0);
  image(img, 0, mouseY * -1);
}
```

NOTE: Remember to include the file extensions *.gif*, *.jpg*, or *.png* when you load the image. Also, be sure that the image name is typed exactly as it appears in the file, including the case of the letters. And if you missed it, read the note earlier in this chapter about making sure that the file extensions are visible on Mac OS X and Windows.

Fonts

Processing can display text in many fonts other than the default. Before you display text in a different typeface, you need to convert one of the fonts on your computer to the VLW format, which stores each letter as a small image. To do this, select Create Font from the Tools menu to open the dialog box (Figure 6-1). Specify the font you want to convert, as well as the size and whether you want it to be smooth (anti-aliased).

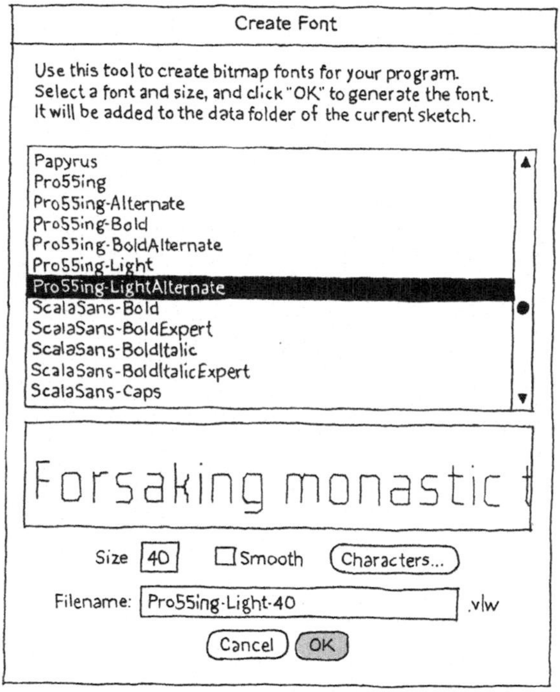

Figure 6-1. Create Font tool.

NOTE: Make the font size selection carefully by considering the following: create the font at the size you want to use it in your sketch (or larger), but keep in mind that larger sizes increase the font file size. Select the Characters option only if you'll be using non-Roman characters like Japanese or Chinese text, because this also increases the file size significantly.

When you click the OK button in the Create Font tool, the VLW font is created and placed in the sketch's *data* folder. Now it's possible to load the font and add words to a sketch. This part is similar to working with images, but there's one extra step:

1. Add the font to the sketch's *data* folder (instructions given previously).

2. Create a *PFont* variable to store the font.

3. Load the font into the variable with *loadFont()*.

4. Use the *textFont()* command to set the current font.

Example 6-6: Drawing with Fonts

Now you can draw these letters to the screen with the *text()* function, and you can change the size with *textSize()*. For this example, you'll need to use the Create Font tool to create a VLW font (and modify the *loadFont()* line to use it), or you can use *AndaleMono-36.vlw* from the *media* folder:

```
PFont font;

void setup() {
  size(480, 120);
  smooth();
  font = loadFont("AndaleMono-36.vlw");
  textFont(font);
}

void draw() {
  background(102);
```

```
  textSize(36);
  text("That's one small step for man...", 25, 60);
  textSize(18);
  text("That's one small step for man...", 27, 90);
}
```

The first parameter to *text()* is the character(s) to draw to the screen.
(Notice that the characters are enclosed within quotes.) The second and
third parameters set the horizontal and vertical location. The location is
relative to the baseline of the text (see Figure 6-2).

Figure 6-2. Typography coordinates.

Example 6-7: Draw Text in a Box

You can also set text to draw inside a box by adding fourth and fifth
parameters that specify the width and height of the box:

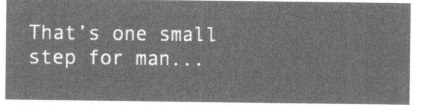

```
PFont font;
void setup() {
  size(480, 120);
  font = loadFont("AndaleMono-24.vlw");
  textFont(font);
}

void draw() {
  background(102);
  text("That's one small step for man...", 26, 30, 240, 100);
}
```

Example 6-8: Store Text in a *String*

In the previous example, the words inside the *text()* function start to make the code difficult to read. We can store these words in a variable to make the code more modular. The *String* data type is used to store text data. Here's a new version of the previous example that uses a *String*:

```
PFont font;
String quote = "That's one small step for man...";

void setup() {
  size(480, 120);
  font = loadFont("AndaleMono-24.vlw");
  textFont(font);
}

void draw() {
  background(102);
  text(quote, 26, 30, 240, 100);
}
```

There's a set of additional functions that affect how letters are displayed on screen. They are explained, with examples, in the Typography category of the Processing Reference.

Shapes

If you make vector shapes in a program like Inkscape or Illustrator, you can load them into Processing directly. This is helpful for shapes you'd rather not build with Processing's drawing functions. As with images, you need to add them to your sketch before they can be loaded.

There are three steps to load and draw an SVG file:

1. Add an SVG file to the sketch's *data* folder.

2. Create a *PShape* variable to store the vector file.

3. Load the vector file into the variable with *loadShape()*.

Example 6-9: Draw with Shapes

After following these steps, you can draw the image to the screen with the *shape()* function:

```
PShape network;

void setup() {
  size(480, 120);
  smooth();
  network = loadShape("network.svg");
}

void draw() {
  background(0);
  shape(network, 30, 10);
  shape(network, 180, 10, 280, 280);
}
```

The parameters for *shape()* are similar to *image()*. The first parameter tells *shape()* which SVG to draw and the next pair sets the position. Optional fourth and fifth parameters set the width and height.

Example 6-10: Scaling Shapes

Unlike raster images, vector shapes can be scaled to any size without losing resolution. In this example, the shape is scaled based on the *mouseX* variable, and the *shapeMode()* function is used to draw the shape from its center, rather than the default position, the upper-left corner:

```
PShape network;

void setup() {
  size(240, 120);
  smooth();
  shapeMode(CENTER);
  network = loadShape("network.svg");
}

void draw() {
  background(0);
  float diameter = map(mouseX, 0, width, 10, 800);
  shape(network, 120, 60, diameter, diameter);
}
```

NOTE: There are limitations to the type of SVG file that you can load. Processing doesn't support all SVG features. See the Processing Reference for PShape for more details.

Robot 4: Media

Unlike the robots created from lines and rectangles drawn in Processing in the previous chapters, these robots were created with a vector drawing program. For some shapes, it's often easier to point and click in a software tool like Inkscape or Illustrator than to define the shapes with coordinates in code.

There's a trade-off to selecting one image creation technique over another. When shapes are defined in Processing, there's more flexibility to modify them while the program is running. If the shapes are defined elsewhere and then loaded into Processing, changes are limited to the position, angle, and size. When loading each robot from an SVG file, as this example shows, the variations featured in Robot 2 (see "Robot 2: Variables" in Chapter 4) are impossible.

Images can be loaded into a program to bring in visuals created in other programs or captured with a camera. With this image in the background, our robots are now exploring for life forms in Norway at the dawn of the 20th century.

The SVG and PNG file used in this example can be downloaded from *http://www.processing.org/learning/books/media.zip.*

```
PShape bot1;
PShape bot2;
PShape bot3;
PImage landscape;

float easing = 0.05;
float offset = 0;

void setup() {
  size(720, 480);
  bot1 = loadShape("robot1.svg");
  bot2 = loadShape("robot2.svg");
  bot3 = loadShape("robot3.svg");
  landscape = loadImage("alpine.png");
  smooth();
}

void draw() {
  // Set the background to the "landscape" image; this image
  // must be the same width and height as the program
  background(landscape);

  // Set the left/right offset and apply easing to make
  // the transition smooth
  float targetOffset = map(mouseY, 0, height, -40, 40);
  offset += (targetOffset - offset) * easing;

  // Draw the left robot
  shape(bot1, 85 + offset, 65);

  // Draw the right robot smaller and give it a smaller offset
  float smallerOffset = offset * 0.7;
  shape(bot2, 510 + smallerOffset, 140, 78, 248);

  // Draw the smallest robot, give it a smaller offset
  smallerOffset *= -0.5;
  shape(bot3, 410 + smallerOffset, 225, 39, 124);
}
```

7/Motion

Like a flip book, animation on screen is created by drawing an image, then drawing a slightly different image, then another, and so on. The illusion of fluid motion is created by *persistence of vision*. When a set of similar images is presented at a fast enough rate, our brains translate these images into motion.

Example 7-1: See the Frame Rate

To create smooth motion, Processing tries to run the code inside *draw()* at 60 frames each second. To confirm the frame rate, run this program and watch the values print to the Console. The *frameRate* variable keeps track of the program's speed.

```
void draw() {
  println(frameRate);
}
```

Example 7-2: Set the Frame Rate

The *frameRate()* function changes the speed at which the program runs. To see the result, uncomment different versions of *frameRate()* in this example:

```
void setup() {
  frameRate(30);     // Thirty frames each second
  //frameRate(12);   // Twelve frames each second
  //frameRate(2);    // Two frames each second
  //frameRate(0.5);  // One frame every two seconds
}
```

```
void draw() {
  println(frameRate);
}
```

NOTE: Processing *tries* to run the code at 60 frames each second, but if it takes longer than 1/60th of a second to run the *draw()* method, then the frame rate will decrease. The *frameRate()* function specifies only the maximum frame rate, and the actual frame rate for any program depends on the computer that is running the code.

Speed and Direction

To create fluid motion examples, we use a data type called *float*. This type of variable stores numbers with decimal places, which provide more resolution for working with motion. For instance, when using *int*s, the slowest you can move each frame is one pixel at a time (1, 2, 3, 4, . . .), but with *float*s, you can move as slowly as you want (1.01, 1.01, 1.02, 1.03, . . .).

Example 7-3: Move a Shape

The following example moves a shape from left to right by updating the *x* variable:

```
int radius = 40;
float x = -radius;
float speed = 0.5;

void setup() {
  size(240, 120);
  smooth();
  ellipseMode(RADIUS);
}
```

```
void draw() {
  background(0);
  x += speed; // Increase the value of x
  arc(x, 60, radius, radius, 0.52, 5.76);
}
```

When you run this code, you'll notice the shape moves off the right of the
screen when the value of the x variable is greater than the width of the
window. The value of x continues to increase, but the shape is no longer
visible.

Example 7-4: Wrap Around

There are many alternatives to this behavior, which you can choose from
according to your preference. First, we'll extend the code to show how to
move the shape back to the left edge of the screen after it disappears off
the right. In this case, picture the screen as a flattened cylinder, with the
shape moving around the outside to return to its starting point:

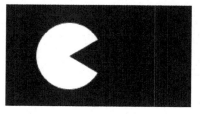 

```
int radius = 40;
float x = -radius;
float speed = 0.5;

void setup() {
  size(240, 120);
  smooth();
  ellipseMode(RADIUS);
}

void draw() {
  background(0);
  x += speed;                // Increase the value of x
  if (x > width+radius) {    // If the shape is off screen,
    x = -radius;             // move to the left edge
  }
  arc(x, 60, radius, radius, 0.52, 5.76);
}
```

On each trip through *draw()*, the code tests to see if the value of *x* has increased beyond the width of the screen (plus the radius of the shape). If it has, we set the value of *x* to a negative value, so that as it continues to increase, it will enter the screen from the left. See Figure 7-1 for a diagram of how it works.

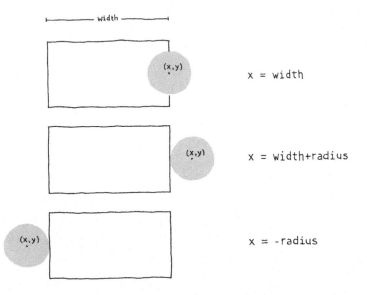

Figure 7-1. *Testing for the left edge of the window.*

Example 7-5: Bounce Off the Wall

In this example, we'll extend Example 7-3 to have the shape change directions when it hits an edge, instead of wrapping around to the left. To make this happen, we add a new variable to store the direction of the shape. A direction value of 1 moves the shape to the right, and a value of −1 moves the shape to the left:

```
int radius = 40;
float x = 110;
float speed = 0.5;
int direction = 1;

void setup() {
  size(240, 120);
  smooth();
  ellipseMode(RADIUS);
}

void draw() {
  background(0);
  x += speed * direction;
  if ((x > width-radius) || (x < radius)) {
    direction = -direction;   // Flip direction
  }
  if (direction == 1) {
    arc(x, 60, radius, radius, 0.52, 5.76); // Face right
  } else {
    arc(x, 60, radius, radius, 3.67, 8.9);  // Face left
  }
}
```

When the shape reaches an edge, this code flips the shape's direction by changing the sign of the *direction* variable. For example, if the *direction* variable is positive when the shape reaches an edge, the code flips it to negative.

Tweening

Sometimes you want to animate a shape to go from one point on screen to another. With a few lines of code, you can set up the start position and the stop position, then calculate the in-between (*tween*) positions at each frame.

Example 7-6: Calculate Tween Positions

To make this example code modular, we've created a group of variables at the top. Run the code a few times and change the values to see how this code can move a shape from any location to any other at a range of speeds. Change the *step* variable to alter the speed:

```
int startX = 20;        // Initial x-coordinate
int stopX = 160;        // Final x-coordinate
int startY = 30;        // Initial y-coordinate
int stopY = 80;         // Final y-coordinate
float x = startX;       // Current x-coordinate
float y = startY;       // Current y-coordinate
float step = 0.005;     // Size of each step (0.0 to 1.0)
float pct = 0.0;        // Percentage traveled (0.0 to 1.0)

void setup() {
  size(240, 120);
  smooth();
}

void draw() {
  background(0);
  if (pct < 1.0) {
    x = startX + ((stopX-startX) * pct);
    y = startY + ((stopY-startY) * pct);
    pct += step;
  }
  ellipse(x, y, 20, 20);
}
```

Random

Unlike the smooth, linear motion common to computer graphics, motion in the physical world is usually idiosyncratic. For instance, think of a leaf floating to the ground, or an ant crawling over rough terrain. We can simulate the unpredictable qualities of the world by generating random numbers. The *random()* function calculates these values; we can set a range to tune the amount of disarray in a program.

Example 7-7: Generate Random Values

The following short example prints random values to the Console, with the range limited by the position of the mouse. The *random()* function always returns a floating-point value, so be sure the variable on the left side of the assignment operator (=) is a *float* as it is here:

```
void draw() {
  float r = random(0, mouseX);
  println(r);
}
```

Example 7-8: Draw Randomly

The following example builds on Example 7-7; it uses the values from *random()* to change the position of lines on screen. When the mouse is at the left of the screen, the change is small; as it moves to the right, the values from *random()* increase and the movement becomes more exaggerated. Because the *random()* function is inside the *for* loop, a new random value is calculated for each point of every line:

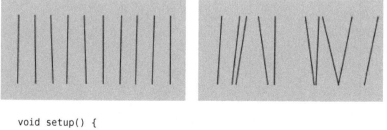

```
void setup() {
  size(240, 120);
  smooth();
}
```

```
void draw() {
  background(204);
  for (int x = 20; x < width; x += 20) {
    float mx = mouseX / 10;
    float offsetA = random(-mx, mx);
    float offsetB = random(-mx, mx);
    line(x + offsetA, 20, x - offsetB, 100);
  }
}
```

Example 7-9: Move Shapes Randomly

When used to move shapes around on screen, random values can
generate images that are more natural in appearance. In the following
example, the position of the circle is modified by random values on each
trip through *draw()*. Because the *background()* function is not used, past
locations are traced:

```
float speed = 2.5;
int diameter = 20;
float x;
float y;

void setup() {
  size(240, 120);
  smooth();
  x = width/2;
  y = height/2;
}

void draw() {
  x += random(-speed, speed);
  y += random(-speed, speed);
  ellipse(x, y, diameter, diameter);
}
```

If you watch this example long enough, you may see the circle leave the window and come back. This is left to chance, but we could add a few *if* structures or use the *constrain()* function to keep the circle from leaving the screen. The *constrain()* function limits a value to a specific range, which can be used to keep *x* and *y* within the boundaries of the display window. By replacing the *draw()* in the preceding code with the following, you'll ensure that the ellipse will remain on the screen:

```
void draw() {
  x += random(-speed, speed);
  y += random(-speed, speed);
  x = constrain(x, 0, width);
  y = constrain(y, 0, height);
  ellipse(x, y, diameter, diameter);
}
```

NOTE: The *randomSeed()* function can be used to force *random()* to produce the same sequence of numbers each time a program is run. This is described further in the Processing Reference.

Timers

Every Processing program counts the amount of time that has passed since it was started. It counts in milliseconds (thousandths of a second), so after 1 second, the counter is at 1,000; after 5 seconds, it's at 5,000; and after 1 minute, it's at 60,000. We can use this counter to trigger animations at specific times. The *millis()* function returns this counter value.

Example 7-10: Time Passes

You can watch the time pass when you run this program:

```
void draw() {
  int timer = millis();
  println(timer);
}
```

Example 7-11: Triggering Timed Events

When paired with an *if* block, the values from *millis()* can be used to sequence animation and events within a program. For instance, after two seconds have elapsed, the code inside the *if* block can trigger a change. In this example, variables called *time1* and *time2* determine when to change the value of the *x* variable:

```
int time1 = 2000;
int time2 = 4000;
float x = 0;

void setup() {
  size(480, 120);
  smooth();
}

void draw() {
  int currentTime = millis();
  background(204);
  if (currentTime > time2) {
    x -= 0.5;
  } else if (currentTime > time1) {
    x += 2;
  }
  ellipse(x, 60, 90, 90);
}
```

Circular

If you're a trigonometry ace, you already know how amazing the sine and cosine functions are. If you're not, we hope the next examples will trigger your interest. We won't discuss the math in detail here, but we'll show a few applications to generate fluid motion.

Figure 7-2 shows a visualization of sine wave values and how they relate to angles. At the top and bottom of the wave, notice how the rate of change (the change on the vertical axis) slows down, stops, then switches direction. It's this quality of the curve that generates interesting motion.

The *sin()* and *cos()* functions in Processing return values between −1 and 1 for the sine or cosine of the specified angle. Like *arc()*, the angles must be given in radian values (see Examples 3-7 and 3-8 for a reminder of how radians work). To be useful for drawing, the *float* values returned by *sin()* and *cos()* are usually multiplied by a larger value.

Figure 7-2. Sine and cosine values.

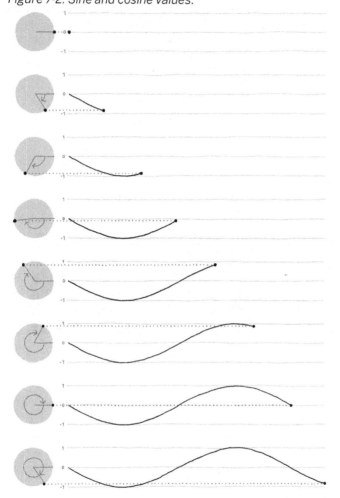

Example 7-12: Sine Wave Values

This example shows how values for *sin()* cycle from –1 to 1 as the angle increases. With the *map()* function, the *sinval* variable is converted from this range to values from 0 and 255. This new value is used to set the background color of the window:

```
float angle = 0.0;

void draw() {
  float sinval = sin(angle);
  println(sinval);
  float gray = map(sinval, -1, 1, 0, 255);
  background(gray);
  angle += 0.1;
}
```

Example 7-13: Sine Wave Movement

This example shows how these values can be converted into movement:

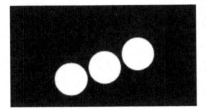 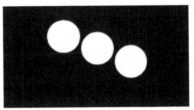

```
float angle = 0.0;
float offset = 60;
float scalar = 40;
float speed = 0.05;

void setup() {
  size(240, 120);
  smooth();
}

void draw() {
  background(0);
  float y1 = offset + sin(angle) * scalar;
  float y2 = offset + sin(angle + 0.4) * scalar;
  float y3 = offset + sin(angle + 0.8) * scalar;
```

```
    ellipse( 80, y1, 40, 40);
    ellipse(120, y2, 40, 40);
    ellipse(160, y3, 40, 40);
    angle += speed;
  }
```

Example 7-14: Circular Motion

When *sin()* and *cos()* are used together, they can produce circular motion.
The *cos()* values provide the x-coordinates, and the *sin()* values the
y-coordinates. Both are multiplied by a variable named *scalar* to change
the radius of the movement and summed with an offset value to set the
center of the circular motion:

```
float angle = 0.0;
float offset = 60;
float scalar = 30;
float speed = 0.05;

void setup() {
  size(120, 120);
  smooth();
}

void draw() {
  float x = offset + cos(angle) * scalar;
  float y = offset + sin(angle) * scalar;
  ellipse( x, y, 40, 40);
  angle += speed;
}
```

Example 7-15: Spirals

A slight change made to increase the *scalar* value at each frame produces
a spiral, rather than a circle:

```
float angle = 0.0;
float offset = 60;
float scalar = 2;
float speed = 0.05;

void setup() {
  size(120, 120);
  fill(0);
  smooth();
}

void draw() {
  float x = offset + cos(angle) * scalar;
  float y = offset + sin(angle) * scalar;
  ellipse( x, y, 2, 2);
  angle += speed;
  scalar += speed;
}
```

Translate, Rotate, Scale

Changing the screen coordinates is an alternative technique to create
motion. For instance, you can move a shape 50 pixels to the right, or you
can move the location of coordinate (0,0) 50 pixels to the right—the visual
result on screen is the same. By modifying the default coordinate system,
we can create different *transformations* including translation, rotation,
and scaling. Figure 7-3 demonstrates this graphically.

```
translate(40, 20);
rect(20, 20, 20, 40);
```

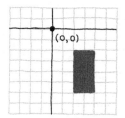

```
translate(60, 70);
rect(20, 20, 20, 40);
```

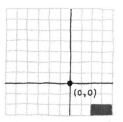

```
rotate(PI/12);
rect(20, 20, 20, 40);
```

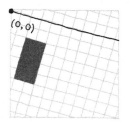

```
rotate(-PI/3);
rect(20, 20, 20, 40);
```

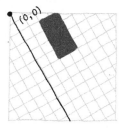

```
scale(1.5);
rect(20, 20, 20, 40);
```

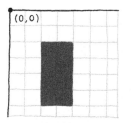

```
scale(3);
rect(20, 20, 20, 40);
```

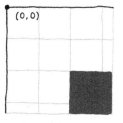

Figure 7-3. Translating, rotating, and scaling the coordinates.

Working with transformations can be tricky, but the *translate()* function is the most straightforward, so we'll start with it. This function can shift the coordinate system left, right, up, and down with its two parameters.

Example 7-16: Translating Location

In this example, notice that each rectangle is drawn at coordinate (0,0), but they are moved around on the screen, because they are affected by *translate()*:

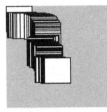 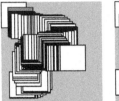 

```
void setup() {
  size(120, 120);
}

void draw() {
  translate(mouseX, mouseY);
  rect(0, 0, 30, 30);
}
```

The *translate()* function sets the (0,0) coordinate of the screen to the mouse location. In the next line, the *rect()* drawn at the new (0,0) is in fact drawn at the mouse location.

Example 7-17: Multiple Translations

After a transformation is made, it is applied to all subsequent drawing functions. Notice what happens when a second *translate* command is added to control a second rectangle:

```
void setup() {
  size(120, 120);
}

void draw() {
  translate(mouseX, mouseY);
  rect(0, 0, 30, 30);
  translate(35, 10);
  rect(0, 0, 15, 15);
}
```

The smaller rectangle was translated the amount of *mouseX* + 35 and
mouseY + 10.

Example 7-18: Isolating Transformations

To isolate the effects of a transformation so they don't affect later
commands, use the *pushMatrix()* and *popMatrix()* functions. When the
pushMatrix() function is run, it saves a copy of the current coordinate
system and then restores that system after *popMatrix()*:

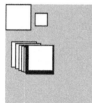 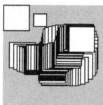 

```
void setup() {
  size(120, 120);
}

void draw() {
  pushMatrix();
  translate(mouseX, mouseY);
  rect(0, 0, 30, 30);
  popMatrix();
  translate(35, 10);
  rect(0, 0, 15, 15);
}
```

In this example, the smaller rectangle always draws in the upper-left corner because the *translate(mouseX, mouseY)* is cancelled by the *popMatrix()*.

NOTE: The *pushMatrix()* and *popMatrix()* functions are always used in pairs. For every *pushMatrix()*, you need to have a matching *popMatrix()*.

Example 7-19: Rotation

The *rotate()* function rotates the coordinate system. It has one parameter, which is the angle (in radians) to rotate. It always rotates relative to (0,0), known as rotating around the *origin*. To spin a shape around its center point, first use *translate()* to move to the location where you'd like the shape, then call *rotate()*, and then draw the shape with its center at coordinate (0,0):

```
float angle = 0.0;

void setup() {
  size(120, 120);
  smooth();
}

void draw() {
  translate(mouseX, mouseY);
  rotate(angle);
  rect(-15, -15, 30, 30);
  angle += 0.1;
}
```

Example 7-20: Combining Transformations

When *translate()* and *rotate()* are combined, the order in which they
appear affects the result. The following example is identical to Example
7-19, except that *translate()* and *rotate()* are reversed. The shape now
rotates around the upper-left corner of the display window, with the
distance from the corner set by *translate()*:

```
float angle = 0.0;

void setup() {
  size(120, 120);
  smooth();
}

void draw() {
  rotate(angle);
  translate(mouseX, mouseY);
  rect(-15, -15, 30, 30);
  angle += 0.1;
}
```

NOTE: You can also use the *rectMode()*, *ellipseMode()*, *imageMode()*, and
shapeMode() functions to make it easier to draw shapes from their center.

Example 7-21: Scaling

The *scale()* function stretches the coordinates on the screen. Like *rotate()*, it transforms from the origin. Therefore, as with *rotate()*, to scale a shape from its center, translate to its location, scale, and then draw with the center at coordinate (0,0):

```
float angle = 0.0;

void setup() {
  size(120, 120);
  smooth();
}

void draw() {
  translate(mouseX, mouseY);
  scale(sin(angle) + 2);
  rect(-15, -15, 30, 30);
  angle += 0.1;
}
```

Example 7-22: Keeping Strokes Consistent

From the thick lines in Example 7-21, you can see how the *scale()* function affects the stroke weight. To maintain a consistent stroke weight as a shape scales, divide the desired stroke weight by the scalar value:

```
float angle = 0.0;

void setup() {
  size(120, 120);
  smooth();
}

void draw() {
  translate(mouseX, mouseY);
  float scalar = sin(angle) + 2;
  scale(scalar);
  strokeWeight(1.0 / scalar);
  rect(-15, -15, 30, 30);
  angle += 0.1;
}
```

Example 7-23: An Articulating Arm

In this final and longest transformation example, we've put together a series of *translate()* and *rotate()* functions to create a linked arm that bends back and forth. Each *translate()* further moves the position of the lines, and each *rotate()* adds to the previous rotation to bend more:

```
float angle = 0.0;
float angleDirection = 1;
float speed = 0.005;

void setup() {
  size(120, 120);
  smooth();
}

void draw() {
  background(204);
  translate(20, 25);   // Move to start position
  rotate(angle);
  strokeWeight(12);
  line(0, 0, 40, 0);
  translate(40, 0);    // Move to next joint
  rotate(angle * 2.0);
  strokeWeight(6);
  line(0, 0, 30, 0);
  translate(30, 0);    // Move to next joint
  rotate(angle * 2.5);
  strokeWeight(3);
  line(0, 0, 20, 0);

  angle += speed * angleDirection;
  if ((angle > QUARTER_PI) || (angle < 0)) {
    angleDirection *= -1;
  }
}
```

Here, we don't use a *pushMatrix()* or *popMatrix()*, because we want the transformations to *propagate*—for each transformation to build on the last. The coordinate system is automatically reset to the default when *draw()* begins each frame.

Robot 5: Motion

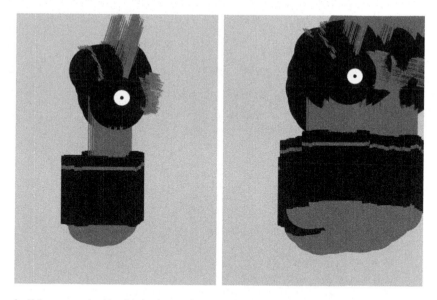

In this example, the techniques for random and circular motion are applied to the robot. The *background()* was removed to make it easier to see how the robot's position and body change.

At each frame, a random number between −4 and 4 is added to the x-coordinate, and a random number between −1 and 1 is added to the y-coordinate. This causes the robot to move more from left to right than top to bottom. Numbers calculated from the *sin()* function change the height of the neck so it oscillates between 50 and 110 pixels high:

```
float x = 180;            // X-coordinate
float y = 400;            // Y-coordinate
float bodyHeight = 153;   // Body height
float neckHeight = 56;    // Neck height
float radius = 45;        // Head radius
float angle = 0.0;        // Angle for motion

void setup() {
  size(360, 480);
  smooth();
  ellipseMode(RADIUS);
  background(204);
}
```

```
void draw() {
  // Change position by a small random amount
  x += random(-4, 4);
  y += random(-1, 1);

  // Change height of neck
  neckHeight = 80 + sin(angle) * 30;
  angle += 0.05;

  // Adjust the height of the head
  float ny = y - bodyHeight - neckHeight - radius;

  // Neck
  stroke(102);
  line(x+2, y-bodyHeight, x+2, ny);
  line(x+12, y-bodyHeight, x+12, ny);
  line(x+22, y-bodyHeight, x+22, ny);
  // Antennae
  line(x+12, ny, x-18, ny-43);
  line(x+12, ny, x+42, ny-99);
  line(x+12, ny, x+78, ny+15);
  // Body
  noStroke();
  fill(102);
  ellipse(x, y-33, 33, 33);
  fill(0);
  rect(x-45, y-bodyHeight, 90, bodyHeight-33);
  fill(102);
  rect(x-45, y-bodyHeight+17, 90, 6);
  // Head
  fill(0);
  ellipse(x+12, ny, radius, radius);
  fill(255);
  ellipse(x+24, ny-6, 14, 14);
  fill(0);
  ellipse(x+24, ny-6, 3, 3);
}
```

8/Functions

Functions are the basic building blocks for Processing programs. They have appeared in every example we've presented. For instance, we've frequently used the *size()* function, the *line()* function, and the *fill()* function. This chapter shows how to write new functions to extend the capabilities of Processing beyond its built-in features.

The power of functions is modularity. Functions are independent software units that are used to build more complex programs—like LEGO® bricks, where each type of brick serves a specific purpose, and making a complex model requires using the different parts together. As with functions, the true power of these bricks is the ability to build many different forms from the same set of elements. The same group of LEGOs that makes a spaceship can be reused to construct a truck, a skyscraper, and many other objects.

Functions are helpful if you want to draw a more complex shape like a tree over and over. The function to draw the tree shape would be made up of Processing's built-in commands, like *line()*, that create the form. After the code to draw the tree is written, you don't need to think about the details of tree drawing again—you can simply write *tree()* (or whatever you named the function) to draw the shape. Functions allow a complex sequence of statements to be abstracted, so you can focus on the higher-level goal (such as drawing a tree), and not the details of the implementation (the *line()* commands that define the tree shape). Once a function is defined, the code inside the function need not be repeated again.

Function Basics

A computer runs a program one line at a time. When a function is run, the computer jumps to where the function is defined and runs the code there, then jumps back to where it left off.

Example 8-1: Roll the Dice

This behavior is illustrated with the *rollDice()* function written for this example. When a program starts, it runs the code in *setup()* and then stops. The program takes a detour and runs the code inside *rollDice()* each time it appears:

```
void setup() {
  println("Ready to roll!");
  rollDice(20);
  rollDice(20);
  rollDice(6);
  println("Finished.");
}

void rollDice(int numSides) {
  int d = 1 + int(random(numSides));
  println("Rolling... " + d);
}
```

The two lines of code in *rollDice()* select a random number between 1 and the number of sides on the dice, and prints that number to the Console. Because the numbers are random, you'll see different numbers each time the program is run:

```
Ready to roll!
Rolling... 20
Rolling... 11
Rolling... 1
Finished.
```

Each time the *rollDice()* function is run inside *setup()*, the code within the function runs from top to bottom, then the program continues on the next line within *setup()*.

The *random()* function (described on page 97) returns a number from 0 up to (but not including) the number specified. So *random(6)* returns a number between 0 and 5.99999.... Because *random()* returns a *float* value, we also use *int()* to convert it to an integer. So *int(random(6))* will return 0, 1, 2, 3, 4, or 5. Then we add 1 so that the number returned is between 1 and 6 (like a die). Like many other cases in this book, counting from 0 makes it easier to use the results of *random()* with other calculations.

Example 8-2: Another Way to Roll

If an equivalent program were written without the *rollDice()* function, it might look like this:

```
void setup() {
  println("Ready to roll!");
  int d1 = 1 + int(random(20));
  println("Rolling... " + d1);
  int d2 = 1 + int(random(20));
  println("Rolling... " + d2);
  int d3 = 1 + int(random(6));
  println("Rolling... " + d3);
  println("Finished.");
}
```

The *rollDice()* function in Example 8-1 makes the code easier to read and maintain. The program is clearer, because the name of the function clearly states its purpose. In this example, we see the *random()* function in *setup()*, but its use is not as obvious. The number of sides on the die is also clearer with a function: when the code says *rollDice(6)*, it's obvious that it's simulating the roll of a six-sided die. Also, Example 8-1 is easier to maintain, because information is not repeated. The phase Rolling... is repeated three times here. If you want to change that text to something else, you would need to update the program in three places, rather than making a single edit inside the *rollDice()* function. In addition, as you'll see in Example 8-5, a function can also make a program much shorter (and therefore easier to maintain and read), which helps reduce the potential number of bugs.

Make a Function

In this section, we'll draw an owl to explain the steps involved in making a function.

Example 8-3: Draw the Owl

First we'll draw the owl without using a function:

```
void setup() {
  size(480, 120);
  smooth();
}

void draw() {
  background(204);
  translate(110, 110);
  stroke(0);
  strokeWeight(70);
  line(0, -35, 0, -65);  // Body
  noStroke();
  fill(255);
  ellipse(-17.5, -65, 35, 35);  // Left eye dome
  ellipse(17.5, -65, 35, 35);   // Right eye dome
  arc(0, -65, 70, 70, 0, PI);   // Chin
  fill(0);
  ellipse(-14, -65, 8, 8); // Left eye
  ellipse(14, -65, 8, 8);  // Right eye
  quad(0, -58, 4, -51, 0, -44, -4, -51);  // Beak
}
```

Notice that *translate()* is used to move the origin (0,0) to 110 pixels over and 110 pixels down. Then the owl is drawn relative to (0,0), with its coordinates sometimes positive and negative as it's centered around the new 0,0 point. See Figure 8-1.

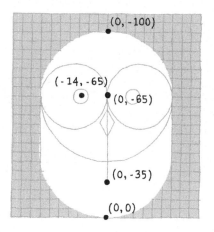

Figure 8-1. The owl's coordinates.

Example 8-4: Two's Company

The code presented in Example 8-3 is reasonable if there is only one owl, but when we draw a second, the length of the code is nearly doubled:

```
void setup() {
  size(480, 120);
  smooth();
}

void draw() {
  background(204);

  // Left owl
  translate(110, 110);
  stroke(0);
  strokeWeight(70);
  line(0, -35, 0, -65);  // Body
```

```
noStroke();
fill(255);
ellipse(-17.5, -65, 35, 35);   // Left eye dome
ellipse(17.5, -65, 35, 35);    // Right eye dome
arc(0, -65, 70, 70, 0, PI);    // Chin
fill(0);
ellipse(-14, -65, 8, 8); // Left eye
ellipse(14, -65, 8, 8);  // Right eye
quad(0, -58, 4, -51, 0, -44, -4, -51); // Beak

// Right owl
translate(70, 0);
stroke(0);
strokeWeight(70);
line(0, -35, 0, -65);   // Body
noStroke();
fill(255);
ellipse(-17.5, -65, 35, 35);   // Left eye dome
ellipse(17.5, -65, 35, 35);    // Right eye dome
arc(0, -65, 70, 70, 0, PI);    // Chin
fill(0);

ellipse(-14, -65, 8, 8);       // Left eye
ellipse(14, -65, 8, 8);        // Right eye
quad(0, -58, 4, -51, 0, -44, -4, -51); // Beak
}
```

The program grew from 21 lines to 34, because the code to draw the first
owl was cut and pasted into the program and a *translate()* was inserted to
move it to the right 70 pixels. This is a tedious and inefficient way to draw
a second owl, not to mention the headache of adding a third owl with this
method. But duplicating the code is unnecessary, because this is the type
of situation where a function can come to the rescue.

Example 8-5: An Owl Function

In this example, a function is introduced to draw two owls with the same
code. If we make the code that draws the owl to the screen into a new
function, the code need only appear once in the program:

```
void setup() {
  size(480, 120);
  smooth();
}

void draw() {
  background(204);
  owl(110, 110);
  owl(180, 110);
}

void owl(int x, int y) {
  pushMatrix();
  translate(x, y);
  stroke(0);
  strokeWeight(70);
  line(0, -35, 0, -65);   // Body
  noStroke();
  fill(255);
  ellipse(-17.5, -65, 35, 35);   // Left eye dome
  ellipse(17.5, -65, 35, 35);    // Right eye dome
  arc(0, -65, 70, 70, 0, PI);    // Chin
  fill(0);
  ellipse(-14, -65, 8, 8);  // Left eye
  ellipse(14, -65, 8, 8);   // Right eye
  quad(0, -58, 4, -51, 0, -44, -4, -51); // Beak
  popMatrix();
}
```

You can see from the illustrations that this example and Example 8-4 have the same result, but this example is shorter, because the code to draw the owl appears only once, inside the aptly named *owl()* function. This code runs twice, because it's called twice inside *draw()*. The owl is drawn in two different locations because of the parameters passed into the function that set the x- and y-coordinates.

Parameters are an important part of functions, because they provide flexibility. We saw another example in the *rollDice()* function; the single parameter named *numSides* made it possible to simulate a 6-sided die, a 20-sided die, or a die with any number of sides. This is just like many other Processing functions. For instance, the parameters to the *line()* function make it possible to draw a line from any pixel on screen to any other pixel. Without the parameters, the function would be able to draw a line only from one fixed point to another.

Each parameter has a data type (such as *int* or *float*), because each parameter is a variable that's created each time the function runs. When this example is run, the first time the owl function is called, the value of the *x* parameter is 110, and *y* is also 110. In the second use of the function, the value of *x* is 180 and *y* is again 110. Each value is passed into the function and then wherever the variable name appears within the function, it's replaced with the incoming value.

Make sure the values passed into a function match the data types of the parameters. For instance, if the following appeared inside the *setup()* for Example 8-5:

```
owl(110.5, 120.2);
```

This would create an error, because the data type for the *x* and *y* parameters is *int*, and the values 110.5 and 120.2 are *float* values.

Example 8-6: Increasing the Surplus Population

Now that we have a basic function to draw the owl at any location, we can draw many owls efficiently by placing the function within a *for* loop and changing the first parameter each time through the loop:

```
void setup() {
  size(480, 120);
  smooth();
}

void draw() {
  background(204);
  for (int x = 35; x < width + 70; x += 70) {
    owl(x, 110);
  }
}


// Insert owl() function from Example 8-5
```

It's possible to keep adding more and more parameters to the function to change different aspects of how the owl is drawn. Values could be passed in to change the owl's color, rotation, scale, or the diameter of its eyes.

Example 8-7: Owls of Different Sizes

In this example, we've added two parameters to change the gray value and size of each owl:

```
void setup() {
  size(480, 120);
  smooth();
}

void draw() {
  background(204);
  randomSeed(0);
  for (int i = 35; i < width + 40; i += 40) {
    int gray = int(random(0, 102));
    float scalar = random(0.25, 1.0);
    owl(i, 110, gray, scalar);
  }
}
```

```
void owl(int x, int y, int g, float s) {
  pushMatrix();
  translate(x, y);
  scale(s);  // Set the size
  stroke(g); // Set the gray value
  strokeWeight(70);
  line(0, -35, 0, -65);  // Body
  noStroke();
  fill(255-g);
  ellipse(-17.5, -65, 35, 35);  // Left eye dome
  ellipse(17.5, -65, 35, 35);   // Right eye dome
  arc(0, -65, 70, 70, 0, PI);   // Chin
  fill(g);
  ellipse(-14, -65, 8, 8); // Left eye
  ellipse(14, -65, 8, 8);  // Right eye
  quad(0, -58, 4, -51, 0, -44, -4, -51); // Beak
  popMatrix();
}
```

Return Values

Functions can make a calculation and then return a value to the main program. We've already used functions of this type, including *random()* and *sin()*. Notice that when this type of function appears, the return value is usually assigned to a variable:

```
float r = random(1, 10);
```

In this case, *random()* returns a value between 1 and 10, which is then assigned to the *r* variable.

A function that returns a value is also frequently used as a parameter to another function. For instance:

```
point(random(width), random(height));
```

In this case, the values from *random()* aren't assigned to a variable—they are passed as parameters to *point()* and used to position the point within the window.

Example 8-8: Return a Value

To make a function that returns a value, replace the keyword *void* with the data type that you want the function to return. In your function, specify the data to be passed back with the keyword *return*. For instance, this example includes a function called *calculateMars()* that calculates the weight of a person or object on our neighboring planet:

```
void setup() {
  float yourWeight = 132;
  float marsWeight = calculateMars(yourWeight);
  println(marsWeight);
}

float calculateMars(float w) {
  float newWeight = w * 0.38;
  return newWeight;
}
```

Notice the data type *float* before the function name to show that it returns a floating-point value, and the last line of the block, which returns the variable *newWeight*. In the second line of *setup()*, that value is assigned to the variable *marsWeight*. (To see your own weight on Mars, change the value of the *yourWeight* variable to your weight.)

Robot 6: Functions

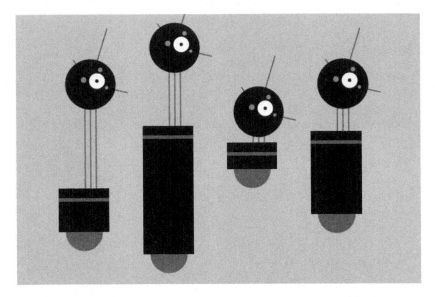

In contrast to Robot 2 (see "Robot 2: Variables" in Chapter 4), this example uses a function to draw four robot variations within the same program. Because the *drawRobot()* function appears four times within *draw()*, the code within the *drawRobot()* block is run four times, each time with a different set of parameters to change the position and height of the robot's body.

Notice how what were global variables in Robot 2 have now been isolated within the *drawRobot()* function. Because these variables apply only to drawing the robot, they belong inside the curly braces that define the *drawRobot()* function block. Because the value of the *radius* variable doesn't change, it need not be a parameter. Instead, it is defined at the beginning of *drawRobot()*:

```
void setup() {
  size(720, 480);
  smooth();
  strokeWeight(2);
  ellipseMode(RADIUS);
}

void draw() {
  background(204);
```

```
  drawRobot(120, 420, 110, 140);
  drawRobot(270, 460, 260, 95);
  drawRobot(420, 310, 80, 10);
  drawRobot(570, 390, 180, 40);
}


void drawRobot(int x, int y, int bodyHeight, int neckHeight) {

  int radius = 45;
  int ny = y - bodyHeight - neckHeight - radius;

  // Neck
  stroke(102);
  line(x+2, y-bodyHeight, x+2, ny);
  line(x+12, y-bodyHeight, x+12, ny);
  line(x+22, y-bodyHeight, x+22, ny);

  // Antennae
  line(x+12, ny, x-18, ny-43);
  line(x+12, ny, x+42, ny-99);
  line(x+12, ny, x+78, ny+15);

  // Body
  noStroke();
  fill(102);
  ellipse(x, y-33, 33, 33);
  fill(0);
  rect(x-45, y-bodyHeight, 90, bodyHeight-33);
  fill(102);
  rect(x-45, y-bodyHeight+17, 90, 6);

  // Head
  fill(0);
  ellipse(x+12, ny, radius, radius);
  fill(255);
  ellipse(x+24, ny-6, 14, 14);
  fill(0);
  ellipse(x+24, ny-6, 3, 3);
  fill(153);
  ellipse(x, ny-8, 5, 5);
  ellipse(x+30, ny-26, 4, 4);
  ellipse(x+41, ny+6, 3, 3);
}
```

9/Objects

Object-oriented programming (OOP) is a different way to think about your programs. Although the term "object-oriented programming" may sound intimidating, there's good news: you've been working with objects since Chapter 6, when you started using *PImage, PFont, String*, and *PShape*. Unlike the primitive data types *boolean, int*, and *float*, which can store only one value, an object can store many. But that's only a part of the story. Objects are also a way to group variables with related functions. Because you already know how to work with variables and functions, objects simply combine what you've already learned into a more understandable package.

Objects are important, because they break up ideas into smaller building blocks. This mirrors the natural world where, for instance, organs are made of tissue, tissue is made of cells, and so on. Similarly, as your code becomes more complicated, you must think in terms of smaller structures that form more complicated ones. It's easier to write and maintain smaller, understandable pieces of code that work together than it is to write one large piece of code that does everything at once.

A software object is a collection of related variables and functions. In the context of objects, a variable is called a *field* (or *instance variable*) and a function is called a *method*. Fields and methods work just like the variables and functions covered in earlier chapters, but we'll use the new terms to emphasize that they are a part of an object. To say it another way, an object combines related data (fields) with related actions and behaviors (methods). The idea is to group together related data with related methods that act on that data.

For instance, to model a radio, think about what parameters can be adjusted and the actions that can affect those parameters:

Fields: *volume, frequency, band* (FM, AM), *power* (on, off)
Methods: *setVolume, setFrequency, setBand*

Modeling a simple mechanical device is easy compared to modeling an organism like an ant or a person. It's not possible to reduce such complex organisms to a few fields and methods, but it is possible to model enough to create an interesting simulation. The *Sims* video game is a clear example. This game is played by managing the daily activities of simulated people. The characters have enough personality to make a playable, addictive game, but no more. In fact, they have only five personality attributes: neat, outgoing, active, playful, and nice. With the knowledge that it's possible to make a highly simplified model of complex organisms, we could start programming an ant with only a few fields and methods:

Fields: *type* (worker, soldier), *weight, length*
Methods: *walk, pinch, releasePheromones, eat*

If you made a list of an ant's fields and methods, you might choose to focus on different aspects of the ant to model. There's no right way to make a model, as long as you make it appropriate for the purpose of your program's goals.

Classes and Objects

Before you can create an object, you must define a class. A *class* is the specification for an object. Using an architectural analogy, a class is like a blueprint for a house, and the object is like the house itself. Each house made from the blueprint can have variations, and the blueprint is only the specification, not a built structure. For example, one house can be blue and the other red; one house might come with a fireplace and the other without. Likewise with objects, the class defines the data types and behaviors, but each object (house) made from a single class (blueprint) has variables (color, fireplace) that are set to different values. To use a more technical term, each object is an *instance* of a class and each instance has its own set of fields and methods.

Define a Class

Before you write a class, we recommend a little planning. Think about what fields and methods your class should have. Do a little brainstorming to imagine all the possible options and then prioritize and make your best guess about what will work. You'll make changes during the programming process, but it's important to have a good start.

For your fields, select clear names and decide the data type for each. The fields inside a class can be any type of data. A class can simultaneously hold many booleans, floats, images, strings, and so on. Keep in mind that one reason to make a class is to group together related data elements. For your methods, select clear names and decide the return values (if any). The methods are used to change the values of the fields and to perform actions based on the fields' values.

For our first class, we'll convert Example 7-9 from earlier in the book. We start by making a list of the fields from the example:

```
float x
float y
int diameter
float speed
```

The next step is to figure out what methods might be useful for the class. In looking at the *draw()* function from the example we're adapting, we see two primary components. The position of the shape is updated and drawn to the screen. Let's create two methods for our class, one for each task:

```
void move()
void display()
```

Neither of these methods return a value, so they both have the return type *void*. When we next write the class based on the lists of fields and methods, we'll follow four steps:

1. Create the block.

2. Add the fields.

3. Write a *constructor* (explained shortly) to assign values to the fields.

4. Add the methods.

First, we create a block:

```
class JitterBug {

}
```

Notice that the keyword *class* is lowercase and the name *JitterBug* is uppercase. Naming the class with an uppercase letter isn't required, but it is a convention (that we strongly encourage) used to denote that it's a class. (The keyword *class*, however, must be lowercase because it's a rule of the programming language.)

Second, we add the fields. When we do this, we have to decide which fields will have their values assigned through a *constructor*, a special method used for that purpose. As a rule of thumb, field values that you want to be different for each class are passed in through the constructor, and the other field values can be defined when they are declared. For the *JitterBug* class, we've decided that the values for *x*, *y*, and *diameter* will be passed in. So the fields are declared as follows:

```
class JitterBug {
    float x;
    float y;
    int diameter;
    float speed = 0.5;
}
```

Third, we add the constructor. The constructor always has the same name as the class. The purpose of the constructor is to assign the initial values to the fields when an object (an instance of the class) is created (Figure 9-1). The code inside the constructor block is run once when the object is first created. As discussed earlier, we're passing in three parameters to the constructor when the object is initialized. Each of the values passed in is assigned to a temporary variable that exists only while the code inside the constructor is run. To clarify this, we've added the name *temp* to each of these variables, but they can be named with any terms that you prefer. They are used only to assign the values to the fields that are a part of the class. Also note that the constructor never returns a value and therefore doesn't have *void* or another data type before it. After adding the constructor, the class looks like this:

```
class JitterBug {

    float x;
    float y;
```

```
  int diameter;
  float speed = 0.5;

  JitterBug(float tempX, float tempY, int tempDiameter) {
    x = tempX;
    y = tempY;
    diameter = tempDiameter;
  }

}
```

The last step is to add the methods. This part is straightforward; it's just like writing functions, but here they are contained within the class. Also, note the code spacing. Every line within the class is indented a few spaces to show that it's inside the block. Within the constructor and the methods, the code is spaced again to clearly show the hierarchy:

```
class JitterBug {

  float x;
  float y;
  int diameter;
  float speed = 2.5;

  JitterBug(float tempX, float tempY, int tempDiameter) {
    x = tempX;
    y = tempY;
    diameter = tempDiameter;
  }

  void move() {
    x += random(-speed, speed);
    y += random(-speed, speed);
  }

  void display() {
    ellipse(x, y, diameter, diameter);
  }

}
```

```
Train red, blue;

void setup() {
  size(400, 400);
  red = new Train("Red Line", 90);
  blue = new Train("Blue Line", 120);
}

class Train {
  String name;
  int distance;
  Train (String tempName, int tempDistance) {
    name = tempName;
    distance = tempDistance;
  }
}
```

Assign "Red Line" to the "name" variable for the "red" object

Assign "90" to the "distance" variable for the "red" object

```
Train red, blue;

void setup() {
  size(400, 400);
  red = new Train("Red Line", 90);
  blue = new Train("Blue Line", 120);
}

class Train {
  String name;
  int distance;
  Train (String tempName, int tempDistance) {
    name = tempName;
    distance = tempDistance;
  }
}
```

Assign "Blue Line" to the "name" variable for the "blue" object

Assign "120" to the "distance" variable for the "blue" object

Figure 9-1. Passing values into the constructor.

Example 9-1: Make an Object

Now that you have defined a class, to use it in a program you must define an object from that class. There are two steps to create an object:

1. Declare the object variable.

2. Create (initialize) the object with the keyword *new*.

We'll start by showing how this works within a Processing sketch and then continue by explaining each part in depth:

```
JitterBug bug;  // Declare object

void setup() {
  size(480, 120);
  smooth();
  // Create object and pass in parameters
  bug = new JitterBug(width/2, height/2, 20);
}

void draw() {
  bug.move();
  bug.display();
}

// Put a copy of the JitterBug class here
```

Each class is a *data type* and each object is a *variable*. We declare object variables in a similar way to variables from primitive data types like *boolean*, *int*, and *float*. The object is declared by stating the data type followed by a name for the variable:

```
JitterBug bug;
```

The second step is to initialize the object with the keyword *new*. It makes space for the object in memory and creates the fields. The name of the constructor is written to the right of the *new* keyword, followed by the parameters into the constructor, if any:

```
JitterBug bug = new JitterBug(200.0, 250.0, 30);
```

The three numbers within the parentheses are the parameters that are passed into the *JitterBug* class constructor. The number of these parameters and their data types must match those of the constructor.

Example 9-2: Making Multiple Objects

In Example 9-1, we see something else new: the period (dot) that's used to access the object's methods inside of *draw()*. The dot operator is used to join the name of the object with its fields and methods. This becomes clearer in this example, where two objects are made from the same class. The *jit.move()* command refers to the *move()* method that belongs to the object named *jit*, and *bug.move()* refers to the *move()* method that belongs to the object named *bug*:

```
JitterBug jit;
JitterBug bug;

void setup() {
  size(480, 120);
  smooth();
  jit = new JitterBug(width * 0.33, height/2, 50);
  bug = new JitterBug(width * 0.66, height/2, 10);
}

void draw() {
  jit.move();
  jit.display();
  bug.move();
  bug.display();
}

// Put a copy of the JitterBug class here
```

Now that the class exists as its own module of code, any changes will modify the objects made from it. For instance, you could add a field to the *JitterBug* class that controls the color, or another that determines its size. These values can be passed in using the constructor or assigned using additional methods, such as *setColor()* or *setSize()*. And because it's a self-contained unit, you can also use the *JitterBug* class in another sketch.

Now is a good time to learn about the tab feature of the Processing Environment (Figure 9-2). Tabs allow you to spread your code across more than one file. This makes longer code easier to edit and more manageable in general. A new tab is usually created for each class, which reinforces the modularity of working with classes and makes the code easy to find.

To create a new tab, click on the arrow at the righthand side of the tab bar. When you select New Tab from the menu, you will be prompted to name the tab within the message window. Using this technique, modify this example's code to try to make a new tab for the *JitterBug* class.

NOTE: Each tab shows up as a separate *.pde* file within the sketch's folder.

```
Processing

(▶)(•)  🔲 🔼 🔽 🔁

[ Ex_09_02 ][ JitterBug ]                                    [➡]

class JitterBug {

    float x;
    float y;
    int diameter;
    float speed = 2.5;

    JitterBug(float tempX, float tempY, int tempDiameter) {
        x = tempX;
        y = tempY;
        diameter = tempDiameter;
    }

    void move() {
        x += random(-speed, speed);
        y += random(-speed, speed);
    }

    void display() {
        ellipse(x, y, diameter, diameter);
    }
}
```

Figure 9-2. Code can be split into different tabs to make it easier to manage.

Robot 7: Objects

A software object combines methods (functions) and fields (variables) into one unit. The *Robot* class in this example defines all of the robot objects that will be created from it. Each *Robot* object has its own set of fields to store a position and the illustration that will draw to the screen. Each has methods to update the position and display the illustration.

The parameters for *bot1* and *bot2* in *setup()* define the x- and y-coordinates and the *.svg* file that will be used to depict the robot. The *tempX* and *tempY* parameters are passed into the constructor and assigned to the *xpos* and *ypos* fields. The *svgName* parameter is used to load the related illustration. The objects (*bot1* and *bot2*) draw at their own location and with a different illustration because they each have unique values passed into the objects through their constructors:

```
Robot bot1;
Robot bot2;

void setup() {
  size(720, 480);
  bot1 = new Robot("robot1.svg", 90, 80);
  bot2 = new Robot("robot2.svg", 440, 30);
  smooth();
}
```

```
void draw() {
  background(204);

  // Update and display first robot
  bot1.update();
  bot1.display();

  // Update and display second robot
  bot2.update();
  bot2.display();
}

class Robot {
  float xpos;
  float ypos;
  float angle;
  PShape botShape;
  float yoffset = 0.0;

  // Set initial values in constructor
  Robot(String svgName, float tempX, float tempY) {
    botShape = loadShape(svgName);
    xpos = tempX;
    ypos = tempY;
    angle = random(0, TWO_PI);
  }

  // Update the fields
  void update() {
    angle += 0.05;
    yoffset = sin(angle) * 20;
  }

  // Draw the robot to the screen
  void display() {
    shape(botShape, xpos, ypos + yoffset);
  }
}
```

10/Arrays

We've introduced new programming ideas in each chapter (variables, functions, objects) and now we've come to the last step—arrays! An *array* is a list of variables that share a common name. Arrays are useful because they make it possible to work with more variables without creating a new name for each. This makes the code shorter, easier to read, and more convenient to update.

Example 10-1: Many Variables

To see what we mean, refer to Example 7-3. This code works fine if we're moving around only one shape, but what if we want to have two? We need to make a new *x* variable and update it within *draw()*:

```
float x1 = -20;
float x2 = 20;

void setup() {
  size(240, 120);
  smooth();
  noStroke();
}
```

```
void draw() {
  background(0);
  x1 += 0.5;
  x2 += 0.5;
  arc(x1, 30, 40, 40, 0.52, 5.76);
  arc(x2, 90, 40, 40, 0.52, 5.76);
}
```

Example 10-2: Too Many Variables

The code for the previous example is still manageable, but what if we want
to have five circles? We need to add three more variables to the two we
already have:

```
float x1 = -10;
float x2 = 10;
float x3 = 35;
float x4 = 18;
float x5 = 30;

void setup() {
  size(240, 120);
  smooth();
  noStroke();
}

void draw() {
  background(0);
  x1 += 0.5;
  x2 += 0.5;
  x3 += 0.5;
  x4 += 0.5;
  x5 += 0.5;
  arc(x1, 20, 20, 20, 0.52, 5.76);
  arc(x2, 40, 20, 20, 0.52, 5.76);
  arc(x3, 60, 20, 20, 0.52, 5.76);
```

```
  arc(x4, 80, 20, 20, 0.52, 5.76);
  arc(x5, 100, 20, 20, 0.52, 5.76);
}
```

This code is starting to get out of control.

Example 10-3: Arrays, Not Variables

Imagine what would happen if you wanted to have 3,000 circles. This would mean creating 3,000 individual variables, then updating each one separately. Could you keep track of that many variables? Would you want to? Instead, we use an array:

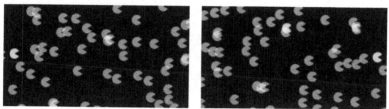

```
float[] x = new float[3000];

void setup() {
  size(240, 120);
  smooth();
  noStroke();
  fill(255, 200);
  for (int i = 0; i < x.length; i++) {
    x[i] = random(-1000, 200);
  }
}

void draw() {
  background(0);
  for (int i = 0; i < x.length; i++) {
    x[i] += 0.5;
    float y = i * 0.4;
    arc(x[i], y, 12, 12, 0.52, 5.76);
  }
}
```

We'll spend the rest of this chapter talking about the details that make this example possible.

Make an Array

Each item in an array is called an *element*, and each has an *index* value to mark its position within the array. Just like coordinates on the screen, index values for an array start counting from 0. For instance, the first element in the array has the index value 0, the second element in the array has the index value 1, and so on. If there are 20 values in the array, the index value of the last element is 19. Figure 10-1 shows the conceptual structure of an array.

```
int[] years = { 1920, 1972, 1980, 1996, 2010 };
```

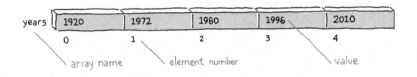

Figure 10-1. An array is a list of one or more variables that share the same name.

Using arrays is similar to working with single variables; it follows the same patterns. As you know, you can make a single integer variable called *x* with this code:

```
int x;
```

To make an array, just place brackets after the data type:

```
int[] x;
```

The beauty of creating an array is the ability to make 2, 10, or 100,000 variable values with only one line of code. For instance, the following line creates an array of 2,000 integer variables:

```
int[] x = new int[2000];
```

You can make arrays from all Processing data types: *boolean, float, String, PShape*, and so on, as well as any user-defined classes. For example, the following code creates an array of 32 *PImage* variables:

```
PImage[] images = new PImage[32];
```

To make an array, start with the name of the data type, followed by the brackets. The name you select for the array is next, followed by the assignment operator (the equal symbol), followed by the *new* keyword, followed by the name of the data type again, with the number of elements to create within the brackets. This pattern works for arrays of all data types.

NOTE: Each array can store only one type of data (*boolean, int, float, PImage*, etc.). You can't mix and match different types of data within a single array. If you need to do this, work with objects instead.

Before we get ahead of ourselves, let's slow down and talk about working with arrays in more detail. Like making an *object*, there are three steps to working with an array:

1. Declare the array and define the data type.

2. Create the array with the keyword *new* and define the length.

3. Assign values to each element.

Each step can happen on its own line, or all the steps can be compressed together. Each of the three following examples shows a different technique to create an array called *x* that stores two integers, 12 and 2. Pay close attention to what happens before *setup()* and what happens within *setup()*.

Example 10-4: Declare and Assign an Array

First we'll declare the array outside of *setup()* and then create and assign the values within. The syntax *x[0]* refers to the first element in the array and *x[1]* is the second:

```
int[] x;              // Declare the array

void setup() {
  size(200, 200);
  x = new int[2];   // Create the array
  x[0] = 12;        // Assign the first value
  x[1] = 2;         // Assign the second value
}
```

Example 10-5: Compact Array Assignment

Here's a slightly more compact example, in which the array is both declared and created on the same line, then the values are assigned within *setup()*:

```
int[] x = new int[2];   // Declare and create the array

void setup() {
  size(200, 200);
  x[0] = 12;            // Assign the first value
  x[1] = 2;             // Assign the second value
}
```

Example 10-6: Assigning to an Array in One Go

You can also assign values to the array when it's created, if it's all part of a single statement:

```
int[] x = { 12, 2 };  // Declare, create, and assign

void setup() {
  size(200, 200);
}
```

NOTE: Avoid creating arrays within *draw()*, because creating a new array on every frame will slow down your frame rate.

Example 10-7: Revisiting the First Example

As a complete example of how to use arrays, we've recoded Example 10-1 here. Although we don't yet see the full benefits revealed in Example 10-3, we do see some important details of how arrays work:

```
float[] x = {-20, 20};

void setup() {
  size(240, 120);
  smooth();
  noStroke();
}

void draw() {
  background(0);
  x[0] += 0.5;  // Increase the first element
  x[1] += 0.5;  // Increase the second element
  arc(x[0], 30, 40, 40, 0.52, 5.76);
  arc(x[1], 90, 40, 40, 0.52, 5.76);
}
```

Repetition and Arrays

The *for* loop, introduced in "Repetition" in Chapter 4, makes it easier to work with large arrays while keeping the code concise. The idea is to write a loop to move through each element of the array one by one. To do this, you need to know the length of the array. The *length* field associated with each array stores the number of elements. We use the name of the array with the dot operator (a period) to access this value. For instance:

```
int[] x = new int[2];      // Declare and create the array
println(x.length);         // Prints 2 to the Console

int[] y = new int[1972];   // Declare and create the array
println(y.length);         // Prints 1972 to the Console
```

Example 10-8: Filling an Array in a *for* Loop

A *for* loop can be used to fill an array with values, or to read the values back out. In this example, the array is first filled with random numbers inside *setup()*, and then these numbers are used to set the stroke value inside *draw()*. Each time the program is run, a new set of random numbers is put into the array:

```
float[] gray;

void setup() {
  size(240, 120);
  gray = new float[width];
  for (int i = 0; i < gray.length; i++) {
    gray[i] = random(0, 255);
  }
}

void draw() {
  for (int i = 0; i < gray.length; i++) {
    stroke(gray[i]);
    line(i, 0, i, height);
  }
}
```

Example 10-9: Track Mouse Movements

In this example, there are two arrays to store the position of the mouse—one for the x-coordinate and one for the y-coordinate. These arrays store the location of the mouse for the previous 60 frames. With each new frame, the oldest x- and y-coordinate values are removed and replaced with the current *mouseX* and *mouseY* values. The new values are added to the first position of the array, but before this happens, each value in the array is moved one position to the right (from back to front) to make room for the new numbers. This example visualizes this action.

Also, at each frame, all 60 coordinates are used to draw a series of ellipses to the screen:

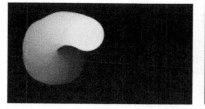 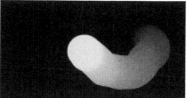

```
int num = 60;
int[] x = new int[num];
int[] y = new int[num];

void setup() {
  size(240, 120);
  smooth();
  noStroke();
}

void draw() {
  background(0);
  // Copy array values from back to front
  for (int i = x.length-1; i > 0; i--) {
    x[i] = x[i-1];
    y[i] = y[i-1];
  }
  x[0] = mouseX;  // Set the first element
  y[0] = mouseY;  // Set the first element
  for (int i = 0; i < x.length; i++) {
    fill(i * 4);
    ellipse(x[i], y[i], 40, 40);
  }
}
```

NOTE: The technique for storing a shifting buffer of numbers in an array shown in this example and Figure 10-2 is less efficient than an alternative technique that uses the % (modulo) operator. This is explained in the Examples→Basics→Input→StoringInput example included with Processing.

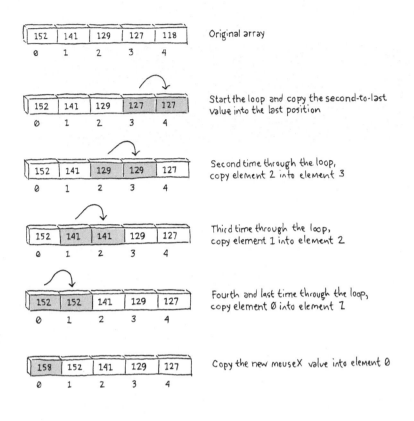

152 | 141 | 129 | 127 | 118   Original array
0   1   2   3   4

152 | 141 | 129 | 127 | 127   Start the loop and copy the second-to-last
0   1   2   3   4   value into the last position

152 | 141 | 129 | 129 | 127   Second time through the loop,
0   1   2   3   4   copy element 2 into element 3

152 | 141 | 141 | 129 | 127   Third time through the loop,
0   1   2   3   4   copy element 1 into element 2

152 | 152 | 141 | 129 | 127   Fourth and last time through the loop,
0   1   2   3   4   copy element 0 into element 1

158 | 152 | 141 | 129 | 127   Copy the new mouseX value into element 0
0   1   2   3   4

Figure 10-2. Shifting the values in an array one place to the right.

Arrays of Objects

The two short examples in this section bring together every major programming concept in this book: variables, iteration, conditionals, functions, objects, and arrays. Making an array of objects is nearly the same as making the arrays we introduced on the previous pages, but there's one additional consideration: because each array element is an object, it must first be created with the keyword *new* (like any other object) before it is assigned to the array. With a custom-defined class such as *JitterBug* (see Chapter 9), this means using *new* to set up each element before it's assigned to the array. Or, for a built-in Processing class such as *PImage*, it means using the *loadImage()* function to create the object before it's assigned.

Example 10-10: Managing Many Objects

This example creates an array of 33 *JitterBug* objects and then updates and displays each one inside *draw()*. For this example to work, you need to add the *JitterBug* class to the code:

```
JitterBug[] bugs = new JitterBug[33];

void setup() {
  size(240, 120);
  smooth();
  for (int i = 0; i < bugs.length; i++) {
    float x = random(width);
    float y = random(height);
    int r = i + 2;
    bugs[i] = new JitterBug(x, y, r);
  }
}

void draw() {
  for (int i = 0; i < bugs.length; i++) {
    bugs[i].move();
    bugs[i].display();
  }
}

// Copy JitterBug class here
```

The final array example loads a sequence of images and stores each as an element within an array of *PImage* objects.

Example 10-11: Sequences of Images

To run this example, get the images from the *media.zip* file as described in Chapter 6. The images are named sequentially (*frame-0000.png*, *frame-0001.png*, and so forth), which makes it possible to create the name of each file within a *for* loop, as seen in the eighth line of the program:

```
int numFrames = 12;   // The number of frames
PImage[] images = new PImage[numFrames];   // Make the array
int currentFrame = 0;

void setup() {
  size(240, 120);
  for (int i = 0; i < images.length; i++) {
    String imageName = "frame-" + nf(i, 4) + ".png";
    images[i] = loadImage(imageName);   // Load each image
  }
  frameRate(24);
}

void draw() {
  image(images[currentFrame], 0, 0);
  currentFrame++;         // Next frame
  if (currentFrame == images.length) {
    currentFrame = 0;   // Return to first frame
  }
}
```

The *nf()* function formats numbers so that *nf(1, 4)* returns the string "0001" and *nf(11, 4)* returns "0011". These values are concatenated with the beginning of the file name ("frame-") and the end (".png") to create the complete file name as a *String* variable. The files are loaded into the array on the following line. The images are displayed to the screen one at a time in *draw()*. When the last image in the array is displayed, the program returns to the beginning of the array and shows the images again in sequence.

Robot 8: Arrays

Arrays make it easier for a program to work with many elements. In this example, an array of *Robot* objects is declared at the top. The array is then allocated inside *setup()*, and each *Robot* object is created inside the *for* loop. In *draw()*, another *for* loop is used to update and display each element of the *bots* array.

The *for* loop and an array make a powerful combination. Notice the subtle differences between the code for this example and Robot 7 (see "Robot 7: Objects" in Chapter 9) in contrast to the extreme changes in the visual result. Once an array is created and a *for* loop is put in place, it's as easy to work with 3 elements as it is 3,000.

The decision to load the SVG file within *setup()* rather than in the *Robot* class is the major change from Robot 7. This choice was made so the file is loaded only once, rather than as many times as there are elements in the array (in this case, 20 times). This change makes the code start faster because loading a file takes time, and it uses less memory because the file is stored once. Each element of the *bot* array references the same file.

```
Robot[] bots;  // Declare array of Robot objects

void setup() {
  size(720, 480);
  PShape robotShape = loadShape("robot1.svg");
  // Create the array of Robot objects
  bots = new Robot[20];
  // Create each object
  for (int i = 0; i < bots.length; i++) {
    // Create a random x-coordinate
    float x = random(-40, width-40);
    // Assign the y-coordinate based on the order
    float y = map(i, 0, bots.length, -100, height-200);
    bots[i] = new Robot(robotShape, x, y);
  }
  smooth();
}

void draw() {
  background(204);
  // Update and display each bot in the array
  for (int i = 0; i < bots.length; i++) {
    bots[i].update();
    bots[i].display();
  }
}

class Robot {
  float xpos;
  float ypos;
  float angle;
  PShape botShape;
  float yoffset = 0.0;

  // Set initial values in constructor
  Robot(PShape shape, float tempX, float tempY) {
    botShape = shape;
    xpos = tempX;
    ypos = tempY;
    angle = random(0, TWO_PI);
  }
```

```
  // Update the fields
  void update() {
    angle += 0.05;
    yoffset = sin(angle) * 20;
  }

  // Draw the robot to the screen
  void display() {
    shape(botShape, xpos, ypos + yoffset);
  }

}
```

11/Extend

This book focuses on using Processing for interactive graphics, because that's the core of what Processing does. However, the software can do much more and is often part of projects that move beyond a single computer screen. For example, Processing has been used to control machines, export images for high-definition films, and export models for 3D printing.

Over the last decade, Processing has been used to make music videos for Radiohead and R.E.M., to make illustrations for publications such as *Nature* and the *New York Times*, to output sculptures for gallery exhibitions, to control a 120×12-foot video wall, to knit sweaters, and much more. Processing has this flexibility because of its system of libraries.

A Processing *library* is a collection of code that extends the software beyond its core functions and classes. Libraries have been important to the growth of the project, because they let developers add new features quickly. As smaller, self-contained projects, libraries are easier to manage than if these features were integrated into the main software.

In addition to the libraries included with Processing (these are called the *core* libraries), there are over 100 *contributed* libraries that are linked from the Processing website. All libraries are listed online at *http://processing. org/reference/libraries/*.

To use a library, select Import Library from the Sketch menu. Choosing a library will add a line of code that indicates that the library will be used with the current sketch. For instance, when the OpenGL Library is added, this line of code is added to the top of the sketch:

```
import processing.opengl.*;
```

Before a contributed library can be imported through the Sketch menu, it must be downloaded from its website and placed within the *libraries* folder on your computer. Your *libraries* folder is located in your sketchbook. You can find the location of your sketchbook by opening the Preferences. Place the downloaded library into a folder within your sketchbook called *libraries*. If this folder doesn't yet exist, create it.

As mentioned, there are more than 100 Processing libraries, so they clearly can't all be discussed here. We've selected a few that we think are fun and useful to introduce in this chapter.

3D

There are two ways to draw in 3D with Processing; both require adding a third parameter to the *size()* function to change the way graphics are drawn. By default, Processing draws using a 2D renderer that is very precise, but slow. This is the *JAVA2D* renderer. A sometimes faster but lower-quality version is *P2D*, the Processing 2D renderer. You can also change the renderer to Processing 3D, called *P3D*, or OpenGL, to allow your programs to draw in one additional dimension, the z-axis (see Figure 11-1).

Render with Processing 3D like this:

```
size(800, 600, P3D);
```

And OpenGL like this:

```
size(800, 600, OPENGL);
```

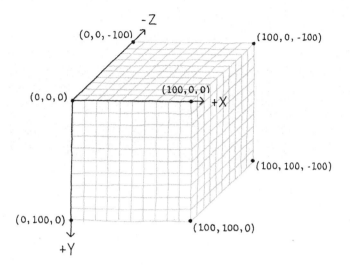

Figure 11-1. Processing's 3D coordinate system.

The *P3D* renderer is built-in, but the OpenGL renderer is a library and requires the *import* statement within the code, as shown at the top of Example 11-1. The OpenGL renderer makes use of faster graphics hardware that's available on most machines sold nowadays.

NOTE: The OpenGL renderer is not guaranteed to be faster in all situations; see the *size()* reference for more details.

Many of the functions introduced in this book have variations for working in 3D. For instance, the basic drawing functions *point()*, *line()*, and *vertex()* simply add z-parameters to the x- and y-parameters that were covered earlier. The transformations *translate()*, *rotate()*, and *scale()* also operate in 3D.

Example 11-1: A 3D Demo

More 3D functions are covered in the Processing Reference, but here's an example to get you started:

```
import processing.opengl.*;

void setup() {
  size(440, 220, OPENGL);
  noStroke();
  fill(255, 190);
}

void draw() {
  background(0);
  translate(width/2, height/2, 0);
  rotateX(mouseX / 200.0);
  rotateY(mouseY / 100.0);
  int dim = 18;
  for (int i = -height/2; i < height/2; i += dim*1.2) {
    for (int j = -height/2; j < height/2; j += dim*1.2) {
      beginShape();
      vertex(i, j, 0);
      vertex(i+dim, j, 0);
      vertex(i+dim, j+dim, -dim);
      vertex(i, j+dim, -dim);
      endShape();
    }
  }
}
```

When you start to work in 3D, new functions are available to explore. It's possible to change the camera, lighting, and material properties, and to draw 3D shapes like spheres and cubes.

Example 11-2: Lighting

This example builds on Example 11-1 by replacing the rectangles with
cubes and adding a few types of lights. Try commenting and uncomment-
ing different lights to see how each works by itself and in combination
with others:

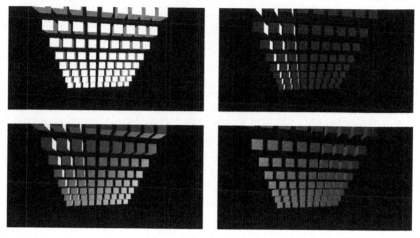

```
import processing.opengl.*;

void setup() {
  size(420, 220, OPENGL);
  noStroke();
  fill(255);
}

void draw() {
  lights();
  //ambientLight(102, 102, 102);
  //directionalLight(255, 255, 255,   // Color
  //                 -1, 0, 0);       // Direction XYZ
  //pointLight(255, 255, 255,         // Color
  //           mouseX, 110, 50);      // Position
  //spotLight(255, 255, 255,          // Color
  //          mouseX, 0, 200,         // Position
  //          0, 0, -1,               // Direction XYZ
  //          PI, 2);                 // Concentration

  rotateY(PI/24);
  background(0);
```

```
translate(width/2, height/2, -20);
int dim = 18;
for (int i = -height/2; i < height/2; i += dim*1.4) {
  for (int j = -height/2; j < height/2; j += dim*1.4) {
    pushMatrix();
    translate(i, j, -j);
    box(dim, dim, dim);
    popMatrix();
  }
}
}
```

There are four types of lights in Processing: spot, point, directional, and ambient. Spot lights radiate in a cone shape; they have a direction, location, and color. Point lights radiate from a single point like a lightbulb of any color. Directional lights project in one direction to create strong lights and darks. Ambient lights create an even light of any color over the entire scene and are almost always used with other lights. The *lights()* function creates a default lighting setup with an ambient and directional light. Lights need to be reset each time through *draw()*, so they should appear at the top of *draw()* to ensure consistent results.

Working in 3D introduces the idea of a "camera" that is pointed at the three-dimensional scene being constructed. Like a real-world camera, it maps the 3D space into the flat 2D plane of the screen. Moving the camera changes the way Processing maps the 3D coordinates of your drawing onto the 2D screen.

Example 11-3: The Processing Camera

By default, Processing creates a camera that points at the center of the screen, therefore shapes away from the center are seen in perspective. The *camera()* function offers control over the camera location, the location at which it's pointed, and the orientation (up, down, tilted). In the following example, the mouse is used to move the location where the camera is pointing:

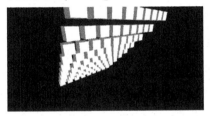
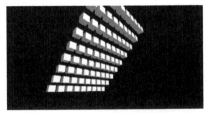

```
import processing.opengl.*;

void setup() {
  size(420, 220, OPENGL);
  noStroke();
}

void draw() {
  lights();
  background(0);
  float camZ = (height/2.0) / tan(PI*60.0 / 360.0);
  camera(mouseX, mouseY, camZ,          // Camera location
         width/2.0, height/2.0, 0,      // Camera target
         0, 1, 0);                      // Camera orientation
  translate(width/2, height/2, -20);
  int dim = 18;
  for (int i = -height/2; i < height/2; i += dim*1.4) {
    for (int j = -height/2; j < height/2; j += dim*1.4) {
      pushMatrix();
      translate(i, j, -j);
      box(dim, dim, dim);
      popMatrix();
    }
  }
}
```

This section has presented the tip of the iceberg of 3D capability. In addition to the core functionality mentioned here, there are many Processing libraries that help with generating 3D forms, loading and exporting 3D shapes, and providing more advanced camera control.

Image Export

The animated images created by a Processing program can be turned
into a file sequence with the *saveFrame()* function. When *saveFrame()* appears at the end of *draw()*, it saves a numbered sequence of TIFF-format
images of the program's output named *screen-0001.tif, screen-0002.tif,*
and so on, to the sketch's folder. These files can be imported into a video
or animation program and saved as a movie file. You can also specify your
own file name and image file format with a line of code like this:

```
saveFrame("output-####.png");
```

NOTE: When using *saveFrame()* inside *draw()*, a new file is saved each
frame—so watch out, as this can quickly fill your *sketch* folder with thousands of files.

Use the # (hash mark) symbol to show where the numbers will appear in
the file name. They are replaced with the actual frame numbers when the
files are saved. You can also specify a subfolder to save the images into,
which is helpful when working with many image frames:

```
saveFrame("frames/output-####.png");
```

Example 11-4: Saving Images

This example shows how to save images by storing enough frames for a
two-second animation. It runs the program at 30 frames per second and
then exits after 60 frames:

```
float x = 0;

void setup() {
  size(720, 480);
  smooth();
  noFill();
  strokeCap(SQUARE);
  frameRate(30);
}

void draw() {
  background(204);
  translate(x, 0);
  for (int y = 40; y < 280; y += 20) {
    line(-260, y, 0, y + 200);
    line(0, y + 200, 260, y);
  }
  if (frameCount < 60) {
    saveFrame("frames/SaveExample-####.tif");
  } else {
    exit();
  }
  x += 2.5;
}
```

Processing will write an image based on the file extension that you use
(*.png*, *.jpg*, or *.tif* are all built in, and some platforms may support others).
A *.tif* image is saved uncompressed, which is fast but takes up a lot of
disk space. Both *.png* and *.jpg* will create smaller files, but because of the
compression, will usually require more time to save, making the sketch
run slowly.

If your output is vector graphics, you can write the output to PDF files for
higher resolution. The PDF Export library makes it possible to write PDF
files directly from a sketch. These vector graphics files can be scaled to any
size without losing resolution, which makes them ideal for print output—
from posters and banners to entire books.

Example 11-5: Draw to a PDF

This example builds on Example 11-4 to draw more chevrons of different weights, but it removes the motion. It creates a PDF file called *Ex-11-5.pdf* because of the third and fourth parameters to *size()*:

```
import processing.pdf.*;

void setup() {
  size(600, 800, PDF, "Ex-11-5.pdf");
  noFill();
  strokeCap(SQUARE);
}

void draw() {
  background(255);
  for (int y = 100; y < height - 300; y+=20) {
    float r = random(0, 102);
    strokeWeight(r / 10);
    beginShape();
    vertex(100, y);
    vertex(width/2, y + 200);
    vertex(width-100, y);
    endShape();
  }
  exit();
}
```

The geometry is not drawn on the screen; it is written directly into the PDF file, which is saved into the sketch's folder. This code in this example runs once and then exits at the end of *draw()*. The resulting output is shown in Figure 11-2.

There are more PDF Export examples included with the Processing software. Look in the *PDF Export* section of the Processing examples to see more techniques.

Figure 11-2. PDF export from Example 11-5.

Hello Arduino

Arduino is an electronics prototyping platform with a series of micro-controller boards and the software to program them. Processing and Arduino share a long history together; they are sister projects with many similar ideas and goals, though they address separate domains. Because they share the same editor and programming environment and a similar syntax, it's easy to move between them and to transfer knowledge about one into the other.

In this section, we focus on reading data into Processing from an Arduino board and then visualize that data on screen. This makes it possible to use new inputs into Processing programs and to allow Arduino programmers to see their sensor input as graphics. These new inputs can be anything that attaches to an Arduino board. These devices range from a distance sensor to a compass or a mesh network of temperature sensors.

This section assumes that you have an Arduino board and that you already have a basic working knowledge of how to use it. If not, you can learn more online at *http://www.arduino.cc* and in the excellent book *Getting Started with Arduino* by Massimo Banzi (O'Reilly). Once you've covered the basics, you can learn more about sending data between Processing and Arduino in another outstanding book, *Making Things Talk* by Tom Igoe (O'Reilly).

Data can be transferred between a Processing sketch and an Arduino board with some help from the Processing Serial Library. *Serial* is a data format that sends one byte at a time. In the world of Arduino, a *byte* is a data type that can store values between 0 and 255; it works like an *int*, but with a much smaller range. Larger numbers are sent by breaking them into a list of bytes and then reassembling them later.

In the following examples, we focus on the Processing side of the relationship and keep the Arduino code simple. We visualize the data coming in from the Arduino board one byte at a time. With the techniques covered in this book and the hundreds of Arduino examples online, we hope this will be enough to get you started.

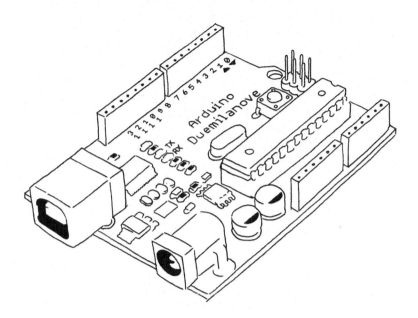

Figure 11-3. An Arduino Duemilanove board.

Example 11-6: Read a Sensor

The following Arduino code is used with the next three Processing examples:

```
// Note: This is code for an Arduino board, not Processing

int sensorPin = 0;      // Select input pin
int val = 0;

void setup() {
  Serial.begin(9600);  // Open serial port
}

void loop() {
  val = analogRead(sensorPin) / 4;  // Read value from sensor
  Serial.print(val, BYTE);          // Print variable to serial port
  delay(100);                       // Wait 100 milliseconds
}
```

There are two important details to note about this Arduino example. First, it requires attaching a sensor into the analog input on pin 0 on the Arduino board. You might use a light sensor (also called a photo resistor, photocell, or light-dependent resistor) or another analog resistor such as a thermistor (temperature-sensitive resistor), flex sensor, or pressure sensor (force-sensitive resistor). The circuit diagram and drawing of the breadboard with components are shown in Figure 11-4. Next, notice that the value returned by the *analogRead()* function is divided by 4 before it's assigned to *val*. The values from *analogRead()* are between 0 and 1023, so we divide by 4 to convert them to the range of 0 to 255 so that the data can be sent in a single byte.

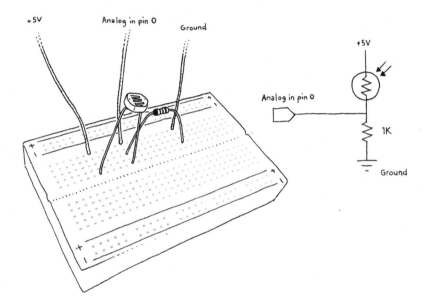

Figure 11-4. Attaching a light sensor to analog in pin 0.

Example 11-7: Read Data from the Serial Port

The first visualization example shows how to read the serial data in from the Arduino board and how to convert that data into the values that fit to the screen dimensions:

```
import processing.serial.*;

Serial port;   // Create object from Serial class
float val;     // Data received from the serial port

void setup() {
  size(440, 220);
  // IMPORTANT NOTE:
  // The first serial port retrieved by Serial.list()
  // should be your Arduino. If not, uncomment the next
  // line by deleting the // before it. Run the sketch
  // again to see a list of serial ports. Then, change
  // the 0 in between [ and ] to the number of the port
  // that your Arduino is connected to.
  //println(Serial.list());
  String arduinoPort = Serial.list()[0];
  port = new Serial(this, arduinoPort, 9600);
}

void draw() {
  if (port.available() > 0) {          // If data is available,
    val = port.read();                 // read it and store it in val
    val = map(val, 0, 255, 0, height); // Convert the value
  }
  rect(40, val-10, 360, 20);
}
```

The Serial library is imported on the first line and the serial port is opened in *setup()*. It may or may not be easy to get your Processing sketch to talk with the Arduino board; it depends on your hardware setup. There is often more than one device that the Processing sketch might try to communicate with. If the code doesn't work the first time, read the comment in *setup()* carefully and follow the instructions.

Within *draw()*, the value is brought into the program with the *read()* method of the Serial object. The program reads the data from the serial port only when a new byte is available. The *available()* method checks to see if a new byte is ready and returns the number of bytes available. This program is written so that a single new byte will be read each time through *draw()*. The *map()* function converts the incoming value from its initial range from 0 to 255 to a range from 0 to the height of the screen; in this program, it's from 0 to 220.

Example 11-8: Visualizing the Data Stream

Now that the data is coming through, we'll visualize it in a more interesting format. The values coming in directly from a sensor are often erratic, and it's useful to smooth them out by averaging them. Here, we present the raw signal from the light sensor illustrated in Figure 11-4 in the top half of the example and the smoothed signal in the bottom half:

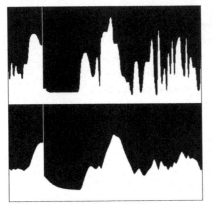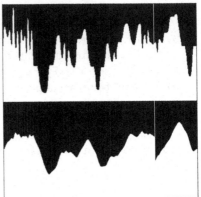

```
import processing.serial.*;

Serial port;   // Create object from Serial class
float val;     // Data received from the serial port
int x;
float easing = 0.05;
float easedVal;

void setup() {
  size(440, 440);
  frameRate(30);
  smooth();
  String arduinoPort = Serial.list()[0];
  port = new Serial(this, arduinoPort, 9600);
  background(0);
}

void draw() {
  if ( port.available() > 0) {        // If data is available,
    val = port.read();                // read it and store it in val
    val = map(val, 0, 255, 0, height); // Convert the values
  }
```

```
  float targetVal = val;
  easedVal += (targetVal - easedVal) * easing;

  stroke(0);
  line(x, 0, x, height);              // Black line
  stroke(255);
  line(x+1, 0, x+1, height);          // White line
  line(x, 220, x, val);               // Raw value
  line(x, 440, x, easedVal + 220);    // Averaged value

  x++;
  if (x > width) {
    x = 0;
  }
}
```

Similar to Examples 5-8 and 5-9, this sketch uses the easing technique. Each new byte from the Arduino board is set as the target value, the difference between the current value and the target value is calculated, and the current value is moved closer to the target. Adjust the *easing* variable to affect the amount of smoothing applied to the incoming values.

Example 11-9: Another Way to Look at the Data

This example is inspired by radar display screens. The values are read in the same way from the Arduino board, but they are visualized in a circular pattern using the *sin()* and *cos()* functions introduced earlier in Examples 7-12 to 7-15:

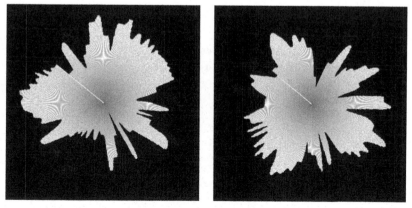

```
import processing.serial.*;

Serial port;   // Create object from Serial class
float val;     // Data received from the serial port
float angle;
float radius;

void setup() {
  size(440, 440);
  frameRate(30);
  strokeWeight(2);
  smooth();
  String arduinoPort = Serial.list()[0];
  port = new Serial(this, arduinoPort, 9600);
  background(0);
}

void draw() {
  if ( port.available() > 0) {  // If data is available,
    val = port.read();          // read it and store it in val
    // Convert the values to set the radius
    radius = map(val, 0, 255, 0, height * 0.45);
  }

  int middleX = width/2;
  int middleY = height/2;
  float x = middleX + cos(angle) * height/2;
  float y = middleY + sin(angle) * height/2;
  stroke(0);
  line(middleX, middleY, x, y);

  x = middleX + cos(angle) * radius;
  y = middleY + sin(angle) * radius;
  stroke(255);
  line(middleX, middleY, x, y);

  angle += 0.01;
}
```

The *angle* variable is updated continuously to move the line drawing the current value around the circle, and the *val* variable scales the length of the moving line to set its distance from the center of the screen. After one time around the circle, the values begin to write on top of the previous data.

We're excited about the potential of using Processing and Arduino together to bridge the world of software and electronics. Unlike the examples printed here, the communication can be bidirectional. Elements on screen can also affect what's happening on the Arduino board. This means you can use a Processing program as an interface between your computer and motors, speakers, lights, cameras, sensors, and almost anything else that can be controlled with an electrical signal. Again, more information about Arduino can be found at *http://www.arduino.cc.*

Community

We've worked hard to make it easy to export Processing programs so that you can share them with others. In the second chapter, we discussed sharing your programs by exporting them. We believe that sharing fosters learning and community. As you modify the programs from this book and start to write your own programs from scratch, we encourage you to review that section of the book and to share your work with others. At the present, the groups at OpenProcessing, Vimeo, Flickr, and the Processing Wiki are exciting places to visit and contribute to. On Twitter, searches for #Processing and Processing.org yield interesting results. These communities are always moving and flowing. Check the main Processing site (*http://www.processing.org*) for fresh links as well as these:

» *http://www.openprocessing.org*

» *http://www.vimeo.com/tag:processing.org*

» *http://www.flickr.com/groups/processing/*

» *http://www.delicious.com/tag/processing.org/*

A/Coding Tips

Coding is a type of writing. Like all types of writing, code has specific rules. For comparison, we'll quickly mention some of the rules for English that you probably haven't thought about in a while because they are second nature. Some of the more invisible rules are writing from left to right and putting a space between each word. More overt rules are spelling conventions, capitalizing the names of people and places, and using punctuation at the end of sentences to provide emphasis! If we break one or more of these rules when writing an email to a friend, the message still gets through. For example, "hello ben. how r u today" communicates nearly as well as, "Hello Ben. How are you today?" However, flexibility with the rules of writing don't transfer to programming. Because you're writing to communicate with a computer, rather than another person, you need to be more precise and careful. One misplaced character is often the difference between a program that runs and one that doesn't.

Processing tries to tell you where you've made mistakes and to guess what the mistake is. When you press the Run button, if there are grammar (syntax) problems with your code (we call them *bugs*), then the Message Area turns red and Processing tries to highlight the line of code that it suspects as the problem. The line of code with the bug is often one line above or below the highlighted line, though in some cases, it's nowhere close. The text in the message area tries to be helpful and suggests the potential problem, but sometimes the message is too cryptic to understand. For a beginner, these error messages can be frustrating. Understand that Processing is a simple piece of software that's trying to be helpful, but it has a limited knowledge of what you're trying to do.

Long error messages are printed to the Console in more detail, and sometimes scrolling through that text can offer a hint. Additionally, Processing can find only one bug at a time. If your program has many bugs, you'll need to keep running the program and fix them one at a time.

Please read and reread the following suggestions carefully to help you write clean code.

Functions and Parameters

Programs are composed of many small parts, which are grouped together to make larger structures. We have a similar system in English: words are grouped into phrases, which are combined to make sentences, which are combined to create paragraphs. The idea is the same in code, but the small parts have different names and behave differently. *Functions* and *parameters* are two important parts. Functions are the basic building blocks of a Processing program. Parameters are values that define how the function behaves.

Consider a function like *background()*. Like the name suggests, it's used to set the background color of the Display Window. The function has three parameters that define the color. These numbers define the red, green, and blue components of the color to define the composite color. For example, the following code draws a blue background:

```
background(51, 102, 153);
```

Look carefully at this single line of code. The key details are the parentheses after the function name that enclose the numbers, the commas between each number, and the semicolon at the end of the line. The semicolon is used like a period. It signifies that one statement is over so the computer can look for the start of the next. All of these parts need to be there for the code to run. Compare the previous example line to these three broken versions of the same line:

```
background 51, 102, 153;   // Error! Missing the parentheses
background(51 102, 153);   // Error! Missing a comma
background(51, 102, 153)   // Error! Missing the semicolon
```

The computer is very unforgiving about even the smallest omission or deviation from what it's expecting. If you remember these parts, you'll have fewer bugs. But if you forget to type them, which we all do, it's not a problem. Processing will alert you about the problem, and when it's fixed, the program will run well.

Color Coding

The Processing environment color-codes different parts of each program. Words that are a part of Processing are drawn as blue and orange to distinguish them from the parts of the program that you invent. The words that are unique to your program, such as your variable and function names, are drawn in black. Basic symbols such as (), [], and > are also black.

Comments

Comments are notes that you write to yourself (or other people) inside the code. You should use them to clarify what the code is doing in plain language and provide additional information such as the title and author of the program. A comment starts with two forward slashes (//) and continues until the end of the line:

```
// This is a one-line comment
```

You can make a multiple-line comment by starting with /* and ending with */. For instance:

```
/*   This comment
     continues for more
     than one line
*/
```

When a comment is correctly typed, the color of the text will turn gray. The entire commented area turns gray so you can clearly see where it begins and ends.

Uppercase and Lowercase

Processing distinguishes uppercase letters from lowercase letters and therefore reads "Hello" as a distinct word from "hello". If you're trying to draw a rectangle with the *rect()* function and you write *Rect()*, the code won't run. You can see if Processing recognizes your intended code by checking the color of the text.

Style

Processing is flexible about how much space is used to format your code. Processing doesn't care if you write:

```
rect(50, 20, 30, 40);
```

or:
```
rect (50,20,30,40);
```

or:
```
rect      (        50,20,
   30,    40)               ;
```

However, it's in your best interest to make the code easy to read. This becomes especially important as the code grows in length. Clean formatting makes the structure of the code immediately legible, and sloppy formatting often obscures problems. Get into the habit of writing clean code. There are many different ways to format the code well, and the way you choose to space things is a personal preference.

Console

The Console is the bottom area of the Processing Environment. You can write messages to the Console with the *println()* function. For example, the following code prints a message followed by the current time:

```
println("Hello Processing.");
println("The time is " + hour() + ":" + minute());
```

The Console is essential to seeing what is happening inside of your programs while they run. It's used to print the value of variables so you can track them, to confirm if events are happening, and to determine where a program is having a problem.

One Step at a Time

We recommend writing a few lines of code at a time and running the code frequently to make sure that bugs don't accumulate without your knowledge. Every ambitious program is written one line at a time. Break your project into simpler subprojects and complete them one at a time so that you can have many small successes, rather than a swarm of bugs. If you have a bug, try to isolate the area of the code where you think the problem lies. Try to think of fixing bugs as solving a mystery or puzzle. If you get stuck or frustrated, take a break to clear your head or ask a friend for help. Sometimes, the answer is right under your nose but requires a second opinion to make it clear.

B/Data Types

There are different categories of data. For instance, think about the data on an ID card. The card has numbers to store weight, height, date of birth, street address, and postal code. It has words to store a person's name and city. There's also image data (a photo) and often an organ donor choice, which is a yes/no decision. In Processing, we have different data types to store each kind of data. Each of the following types is explained in more detail elsewhere in the book, but this is a summary.

Name	Description	Range of values
int	Integers (whole numbers)	−2,147,483,648 to 2,147,483,647
float	Floating-point values	−3.40282347E+38 to 3.40282347E+38
boolean	Logical value	true or false
char	Single character	A–z, 0–9, and symbols
String	Sequence of characters	Any letter, word, sentence, and so on
PImage	PNG, JPG, or GIF image	N/A
PFont	VLW font; use the Create Font tool to make	N/A
PShape	SVG file	N/A

As a guideline, a *float* number has about four digits of accuracy after the decimal point. If you're counting or taking small steps, you should use an *int* value to take the steps, and then perhaps scale it by a *float* if necessary when putting it to use.

There are more data types than those mentioned here, but these are the most useful for the work typically made with Processing. In fact, as mentioned in Chapter 9, there are infinite types of data, because every new class is a different data type.

C/Order of Operations

When mathematical calculations are performed in a program, each operation takes place according to a prespecified order. This *order of operations* ensures that the code is run the same way every time. This is no different from arithmetic or algebra, but programming has other operators that are less familiar.

In the following table, the operators on the top are run before those below. Therefore, an operation inside parentheses will run first and an assignment will run last.

Name	Symbol	Examples
Parentheses	()	a * (b + c)
Postfix, Unary	++ -- !	a++ --b !c
Multiplicative	* / %	a * b
Additive	+ -	a + b
Relational	> < <= >=	if (a > b)
Equality	== !=	if (a == b)
Logical AND	&&	if (mousePressed && (a > b))
Logical OR	||	if (mousePressed || (a > b))
Assignment	= += -= *= /= %=	a = 44

D/Variable Scope

The rule of variable scope is defined simply: a variable created inside a block (code enclosed within braces: { and }) exists only inside that block. This means that a variable created inside *setup()* can be used only within the *setup()* block, and likewise, a variable declared inside *draw()* can be used only inside the *draw()* block. The exception to this rule is a variable declared outside of *setup()* and *draw()*. These variables can be used in both *setup()* and *draw()* (or inside any other function that you create). Think of the area outside of *setup()* and *draw()* as an implied code block. We call these variables *global variables*, because they can be used anywhere within the program. We call a variable that is used only within a single block a *local variable*. Following are a couple of code examples that further explain the concept. First:

```
int i = 12;     // Declare global variable i and assign 12

void setup() {
  size(480, 320);
  int i = 24;   // Declare local variable i and assign 24
  println(i);   // Prints 24 to the console
}

void draw() {
  println(i);   // Prints 12 to the console
}
```

And second:

```
void setup() {
  size(480, 320);
  int i = 24;   // Declare local variable i and assign 24
}

void draw() {
  println(i);   // ERROR! The variable i is local to setup()
}
```

Index

E

easing
   mouse movements, 56–57
   smoothing lines with, 57
elements, defined (arrays), 144
ellipses
   drawing, 9, 19–20
   ellipseMode() function, 25
else blocks, 62–63
embedded for loops, 46
endShape() function, 30
examples and reference (Processing), 13–14
exporting
   images, 164–167
   sketches, 12–13
expressions, arithmetic, 41–42

F

fields, object, 129–134
fill() function, 26
float data type, 92
float numbers, 183
folders, library, 158
fonts
   creating, 83–84
   drawing with, 84–85
for loops
   examples of, 42–47
   filling arrays with values in, 148
frame rates, 91–92
functions
   basics of, 116–117
   calculating and returning values with, 124–125
   coding tips, 178
   defined, 15
   steps for creating, 118–124

G

Getting Started with Arduino (O'Reilly), 168
GIF image format, 12, 81–82
GIMP software, 81
global variables, 52
gray values, 27–28

H

HTML files in applet folder, 12

I

if blocks, 62–63
images
   drawing to screen, 78–80
   exporting, 164–167
   image() function, 79
   resizing, 80–81
   saving, 164–165
initialization statement, 44
instances, defined (objects), 130
instance variables, 129

J

JAR file in applet folder, 12
JAVA2D renderer, 158
JPEG image format, 81–82

K

keyboard characters, setting size of, 71
keyCode variable, 73
keyPressed variable, 68–70
keys
   detecting specific, 72–73
   tapping, 70–71

L

libraries, Processing, 157–158
lighting in 3D (example), 161–162
lights() function, 162
lines
   drawing, 18
   drawing continuous, 55
   drawing smooth, 23–24
   and pins, creating, 48
   setting thickness of, 55–56
   smoothing with easing, 57
Linux, installing Processing on, 7–8
loadFont() function, 84
loadImage() function, 78

R

radians
    defined, 20–21
    drawing with, 22
random() function, 97, 113–114, 117
randomSeed() function, 99
ranges, mapping values to, 58–59
raster images in JPEG/PNG/GIF formats, 81
reading sensors (Arduino), 169–170
rectangles
    cursor position relative to, 67–68
    drawing, 19
rectMode() function, 25
Reference and examples (Processing), 14
relational operators, 44
resizing images, 80–81
RGB color, 28
robot programs (examples)
    arrays of Robot objects, 153–155
    drawing P5 robot, 34–35
    drawRobot() function, 126–128
    loading images from SVG/PNG files, 89–90
    modifying code with variables, 49–50
    random and circular movements, 113–114
    Robot class and objects, 138–139
    shapes responding to mouse, 74–76
rotate() function, 108
rotating coordinate system, 108–109
rows and columns, creating with for loops, 47
Run button, 10–11

S

Safari Books Online, xi
saving
    images, 164–165
    Save command, 11–12
    saveFrame() function, 164
scale() function, 110
scaling shapes, 88, 110–113

scope, variable, 187
sensors, reading (Arduino), 169–170
Serial Library (Processing), 168, 171
setup() function, 52–53
shapes
    custom, 30–33
    drawing basic, 16–18
    drawing randomly, 97–99
    drawing with, 87
    moving, 92–93
    properties, 23–25
    responding to mouse, 74–75
    scaling, 88
    shape() function, 87
shortcuts for calculations, 42
sin() and cos() functions, 101–104
sine wave values/movement, 102–103
size() function, 15–16, 40
sketching
    creating/saving sketches, 11–12
    exporting sketches, 12–13
    overview, 2
    sketchbook, defined, 11
    Sketch menu, 11
smoothing lines with easing, 57
smooth lines, drawing, 23–24
spirals, creating, 104
spot lights, 162
strings, storing text in, 86
strokeCap() function, 25
stroke() function, 26
strokeJoin() function, 25
stroke weights
    consistency of, 111–112
    setting, 24
style tips for coding, 180
SVG files, loading and drawing, 87
SVG format, vector shapes in, 81
syntax, precise use of, 9

T

tab feature (Processing Environment), 137
tapping keys, 70–71
test statement, 44

About the Authors

Casey Reas is a professor in the Department of Design Media Arts at UCLA and a graduate of the MIT Media Laboratory. Reas's software has been featured in numerous solo and group exhibitions at museums and galleries in the United States, Europe, and Asia. With Ben Fry, he cofounded Processing in 2001. He is the coauthor of *Processing: A Programming Handbook for Visual Designers and Artists* (MIT Press, 2007) and *Form+Code in Design, Art, and Architecture* (Princeton Architectural Press, 2010). His work is archived at *www.reas.com*.

Ben Fry has a doctorate from the MIT Media Laboratory and was the 2006–2007 Nierenberg Chair of Design for the Carnegie Mellon School of Design. He worked with Casey Reas to develop Processing, which won a Golden Nica from the Prix Ars Electronica in 2005. Fry's work has received a New Media Fellowship from the Rockefeller Foundation, and been shown at the Museum of Modern Art, Ars Electronica, the 2002 Whitney Biennial, and the 2003 Cooper Hewitt Design Triennial.

Colophon

The cover, heading, and body font is BentonSans, and the code font is Bitstreams Vera Sans Mono.

CPSIA information can be obtained at www.ICGtesting.com
Printed in the USA
BVOW08s0155290515

402167BV00008B/6/P